WITHDRAWAL

WITHDRAWAL

Early Childhood Practice
Froebel Today

Education at SAGE

SAGE is a leading international publisher of journals, books, and electronic media for academic, educational, and professional markets.

Our education publishing includes:

- accessible and comprehensive texts for aspiring education professionals and practitioners looking to further their careers through continuing professional development

- inspirational advice and guidance for the classroom

- authoritative state of the art reference from the leading authors in the field

Find out more at: **www.sagepub.co.uk/education**

Early Childhood Practice
Froebel Today

Edited by **Tina Bruce**

Los Angeles | London | New Delhi
Singapore | Washington DC

First published 2012

SAGE Publications Ltd
1 Oliver's Yard
55 City Road
London EC1Y 1SP

SAGE Publications Inc.
2455 Teller Road
Thousand Oaks, California 91320

SAGE Publications India Pvt Ltd
B 1/I 1 Mohan Cooperative Industrial Area
Mathura Road
New Delhi 110 044

SAGE Publications Asia-Pacific Pte Ltd
3 Church Street
#10-04 Samsung Hub
Singapore 049483

Library of Congress Control Number: 2011934078

British Library Cataloguing in Publication data

A catalogue record for this book is available from the British Library

ISBN 978-1-4462-1124-3
ISBN 978-1-4462-1125-0 (pbk)

Typeset by C&M Digitals (P) Ltd, Chennai, India
Printed in India at Replika Press Pvt Ltd
Printed on paper from sustainable resources

CONTENTS

About the authors   vii
Preface   xi
    Professor Maurice Craft, PhD, DLitt
    Councillor Marilyne MacLaren   xii
Acknowledgements   xiv

Introduction   1
Professor Tina Bruce

1 The whole child   5
    Tina Bruce

2 Family, community and the wider world   17
    Tina Bruce

3 The changing of the seasons in the Child Garden   29
    Stella Brown

4 Adventurous and challenging play outdoors   43
    Helen Tovey

5 Offering children first-hand experiences through forest school: relating to and learning about nature   57
Lynn McNair

6 The time-honoured Froebelian tradition of learning out of doors   69
Jane Read

7 Family songs in the Froebelian tradition   81
Maureen Baker

8 The importance of hand and finger rhymes: a Froebelian approach to early literacy   95
Jenny Spratt

9 Froebel's Mother Songs today   107
Marjorie Ouvry

10 Gifts and Occupations: Froebel's Gifts (wooden block play) and Occupations (construction and workshop experiences) today   121
Jane Whinnett

11 Froebelian methods in the modern world: a case of cooking   137
Chris McCormick

12 Bringing together Froebelian principles and practices   155
Tina Bruce

Integrated book list and bibliography   161
Index   169

ABOUT THE AUTHORS

Professor Tina Bruce CBE Tina is a Froebel trained teacher (Froebel Educational Institute, now part of the University of Roehampton). She trained at the University of Manchester to teach children with hearing impairments, and has taught in both mainstream and special schools. She was Head of the Froebel Research Nursery School working with Chris Athey (Research Fellow) before joining the staff of the Froebel College, where she became Director of the Centre for Early Childhood Studies at the University. She has worked with the British Council in Egypt, New Zealand and British schools in China and Egypt. She has written many books and articles, and spoken at conferences internationally and in the UK. She was awarded International Woman Scholar by the University of Virginia Commonwealth. She is a Vice-President of BAECE: Early Education.

Maureen Baker MBE Maureen is a trained teacher tutored by Sheena Johnstone, a leading Froebelian, and Margaret Cameron at Moray House now part of the University of Edinburgh. She recently retired from Headship of the outstanding nursery school, 'Children's House' one of the pioneering nursery schools in Scotland with a national reputation for its excellence in both early education and care and for its work in the community in Edinburgh. Sadly the school no longer exists having been integrated into a campus model.

Maureen's invaluable expertise has been a crucial contribution in developing the Froebel Edinburgh Network, in the organisation of the well established conferences and giving quiet backstage support to the team.

Stella Brown   Stella is Headteacher of Tynecastle Nursery School in Edinburgh, which has recently expanded and continues to show great quality of practice. She undertook the Froebel training at Jordanhill, Glasgow, and leads and co-ordinates the Nursery Headteachers' Group in the City of Edinburgh. She is a committee member of the Froebel Edinburgh Network, the group which has pioneered the establishment of conferences examining the usefulness of Froebel's approach today. This led to her becoming part of the teaching team for the part-time Froebel Certificate Course at the University of Edinburgh, providing a practical work component which is taught in the school.

Chris McCormick   Chris is Headteacher of Cameron House Nursery School in Edinburgh, which has recently expanded. This was a pioneer nursery school in Edinburgh, and has a time-honoured tradition of excellence. She qualified at Moray House, now part of the University of Edinburgh, as a Froebel trained teacher. She has worked in leadership roles in developing community schools. She is a member of the committee of the Froebel Edinburgh Network, contributing to the organisation of conferences in Edinburgh, exploring the Froebel approach today. She teaches on the Froebel Certificate Course in Edinburgh with practical experience undertaken at Cameron House Nursery School.

Lynn McNair OBE   Lynn is Head of the Cowgate Under 5s Centre in Edinburgh. The Froebel Certificate at the University of Roehampton helped her to articulate in lectures and publications her intuitive Froebelian practice. Cowgate was judged the most outstanding in Scotland by the HMIE Inspectors. She is a member of the Froebel Edinburgh Network which sets up conferences emphasising Froebelian practice today. She leads the part-time Early Childhood Studies Degree at the University of Edinburgh, and with Dr John Davis and Jane Whinnett developed the Froebel Certificate at the University, where she is the Course Leader.

Marjorie Ouvry   Marjorie trained and worked as a Froebel teacher in Aberdeen before gaining her Masters degree from the University of London. She has lectured in child development and education and was head teacher of two inner-city schools, one of them the famous Rachel McMillan Nursery School in Deptford. She now undertakes consultancy and training in early years education. She is particularly interested in play, outdoor learning, music and movement. She taught on the Froebel Certificate Course at the University of Roehampton and is the External Examiner for the Froebel Certificate Course at the University of Edinburgh, and speaks at national conferences. She is also a professionally trained singer, (Trinity College of Music) and, to the delight of the audience, sang one of the Froebel Mother Songs at a Conference in Edinburgh. She is an Associate of Early Education with whom she has published one of her books – *Sounds like Playing* the other *Exercising Muscles and Minds* is published by National Children's Bureau.

Jane Read   Jane was the greatly-valued Archivist at the Froebel Educational Institute, now part of the university of Roehampton. She joined the lecturing staff of the university, making an important contribution in her teaching and research on Froebel and the work of other pioneer educators. She has published widely in academic journals, and contributed chapters in books for practitioners, reaching a wide and diverse audience. She was a key person in the successful development and establishment of the Froebel Certificate Course at the University of Roehampton, and was the course leader. She teaches on the University of Edinburgh Froebel Certificate Course and has spoken at Froebel Conferences and other major educational research conferences in the UK and overseas.

Jenny Spratt   Jenny has recently retired from leading the consistently outstanding Peterborough Local Authority Early Years and Childcare Team. She is an early years Sector Specialist for the Centre for Excellence and Outcomes (C4EO) and in other consultancy contexts. She was a member of the Ministerial Advisory Group on Early Childhood Education, developing the 'Curriculum Guidance for the Foundation Stage', EYFS, and the Tickell Review. She is co-author of *Essentials of Literacy from 0–7: A Whole-Child Approach to Communication, Language and Literacy* and has contributed to other books and articles. She speaks at conferences, including Nursery World and the Edinburgh Froebel Conference.

Helen Tovey   Helen is Principal Lecturer at the University of Roehampton. She trained at the Froebel Educational Institute and became head of Somerset Nursery school which was described as a jewel in the crown of the London maintained nursery schools, particularly highly regarded for its work in science and outdoor learning. She joined the staff at the University of Roehampton where she has developed her work on risk, adventure and challenge in the outdoor learning environment. Her book *Playing Outdoors: Spaces and Places, Risk and Challenge* is widely used and much quoted, combining practice, research and theory in the Froebelian tradition. She teaches on the Froebel Certificate in Edinburgh, and speaks at many conferences, including the Canterbury Christ Church University Conference, 'A Froebelian exploration of outdoor play and Learning'.

Jane Whinnett   Jane qualified as a Froebel trained teacher at Moray House, now part of the University of Edinburgh. She is Headteacher of Balgreen Nursery School in Edinburgh, which has a sustained history of quality. She has been a major contributor and leader in the establishment of the Edinburgh Froebel Network, organising conferences and in developing the Froebel course at the University of Edinburgh with Lynn McNair and Dr John Davis. She is now a lead tutor in teaching the course, which includes lecturing, seminars and contributing through practical experience undertaken at Balgreen Nursery School. She was, until recently, a Trustee of BAECE: Early Education. She has published articles and contributed to articles in the Scottish *Times Educational Supplement*.

PREFACE

This volume on Froebelian practice in the twenty-first century is developed from contributions to several very successful recent conferences at Edinburgh University and the University of Roehampton, London, which brought together many practising teachers, classroom assistants and others to discuss issues relating to learning in very young children. Two of the conferences were supported by the Incorporated Froebel Educational Institute (IFEI) in London, a charity established in the 1890s to promote early childhood education, including teacher training and also research, building on the work of Friedrich Froebel. Further such conferences are envisaged, and IFEI is currently engaged in a range of activities to support and enhance the learning of young children in the UK and overseas.

There can be little doubt that the education of the very young provides an essential foundation for all that follows, and the nature of that education is critical. The IFEI hopes that the work of these conferences has been of value, and that readers will find much of interest in the pages which follow.

Professor Maurice Craft, PhD, DLitt
Chair, IFEI Education Working Group

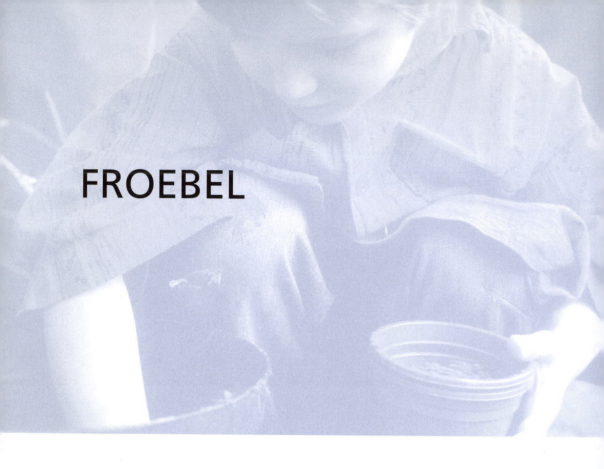

FROEBEL

Froebel is a man whose time has indeed come. His philosophy and ideas have a real resonance with Scotland's new *Curriculum for Excellence* and other Early Years developments. Recent academic work has shown the importance of the first three years of life and its impact and influence on the physical development of a child's brain. This has reinforced and highlighted Froebel's own pedagogy.

Part of the emotional appeal of Froebel is that he is keen to allow children to be children. He enforces their natural curiosity, the innocent joy and fun of play, the desire to learn and to be creative. In an increasingly complex, technical, materialistic and highly commercialised world, I find this comforting. Froebel's emphasis on activity and development is particularly relevant to today's educationalists, when we have so many children who sit at home and become couch potatoes. While we live in an environment where parents are frightened to let children go, to experience the outside world, to explore, we, in our Early Years programme, have a duty to balance this fear by giving children freedom and opportunity to learn for themselves.

The importance of play, interactive and personalised learning, the importance of all things natural, of nurturing a child's creative talents and of allowing children to take risks are all part of the rich and warming learning experience that is a Froebelian nursery.

For all these reasons I am so delighted to have seen the return to Edinburgh of the only Froebelian training course in Scotland – in partnership with the universities of Edinburgh and Roehampton. The courses have been open to all those working in Early Years and have been heavily over-subscribed. For me, one of the most exciting developments has been the inclusion of primary teachers on the course, who have applied Froebelian principles and practice to their older children – with transforming results.

We have a great tradition of Early Years education and development in Edinburgh and Scotland and I am proud to say that Froebel underpins Edinburgh's Early Years strategy and Action Plan.

It is to the credit of a small number of dedicated and enthusiastic Edinburgh Early Years practitioners (who are contributors to this book) that we have the new course available and I am very proud of their achievement in this city.

Councillor Marilyne MacLaren

ACKNOWLEDGEMENTS

The authors of this book would like to express appreciation to Dr John Davis (University of Edinburgh) whose encouragement in setting up the Froebel Certificate at the University of Edinburgh was of central importance. Thanks also to Marilyne MacLaren for her stalwart support in this.

The authors would also like to thank the following people for their practical help in the process of developing this book: Lockhart Geddes and Jill Pirres.

Thanks also to Marianne Lagrange, Kathryn Bromwich, Jeanette Graham and Nicola Marshall from Sage and the production team including Beth Crockett.

For contributing photographs – thanks to the children, parents and staff as follows:

Maureen Baker
Heartfelt thanks to wee Sylvie my grand daughter and her brother Jordan for being such a joy to observe and to my daughters Pamela and Louise for their support. Thanks also to Pamela and Stephen for giving me permission to use photographs of their daughter, Sylvie Grace. A special thanks to Tina Bruce for her endless support of the Froebel Network Edinburgh and for making the book happen.

Stella Brown
First, special thanks to my husband, Graeme, and daughters, Katie and Nicola, for their love, care and encouragement. Their unfailing support and good humour have given me the confidence to share my knowledge, ideas and experiences in this book. My colleagues at Tynecastle Nursery School work tirelessly with children and families in our 'oasis' in the city of Edinburgh and I thank them sincerely for their friendship and belief in me as leader of learning. Sincere thanks to Professor Tina Bruce for her knowledge, wisdom and integrity. Without her trust and belief in the work of the group this book would not have been possible.

Chris McCormick
I would like to express thanks to Fatimah and her family, and to acknowledge the ongoing work of children, parents and staff of Cameron House Nursery School.

Lynn McNair
I would like to acknowledge the children, parents and staff at Cowgate under 5s Centre.
Fondest memories of my brother, Jacky (9 April 1954 to 13 July 2011) with whom I shared many childhood memories playing outdoors.

Marjorie Ouvry
I would like to acknowledge the Edinburgh Froebel Network for their dedicated work in promoting good practice in nursery and early years education and particularly inspiring me.

Jane Read
Thanks to the Froebel Early Childhood Collection at the University of Roehampton for the photographs in the chapter by Jane Read.

Jenny Spratt
I would like to thank William's parents for allowing him to be used as a focus of my talk in Edinburgh and in this chapter.

Helen Tovey
My thanks to staff and children at Bayonne Nursery School, London, for permission to use photographs of play outdoors.

Jane Whinnett
I would like to thank the children, parents and staff of Balgreen Nursery School; Douglas, my family and friends who support me to do the job I love; and Tina Bruce whose leadership has empowered all of us to think we did it all by ourselves.

INTRODUCTION

Tina Bruce

Friedrich Froebel – who is he? That is often the response of younger students and practitioners of early childhood education. In fact, his influence and the impact of his work is deeply embedded in practice both in the UK and in other countries of the world.

In this book, the authors explore and reflect on the ways in which Froebel continues to be a resource for practitioners today. He was not a Romantic, as is sometimes suggested, because he believed that each unique and individual child is part of the whole, through family, community and eventually to the vastness of the universe.

The first and second chapters explore the important resource Froebel has left us in the way he sees the whole child in the family and wider world. His approach was holistic.

In the next chapters, the learning that becomes important through spending time in gardens and forests becomes the focus. These chapters resonate with Froebel's belief in the importance of understanding nature as part of a child's education. Stella Brown, Helen Tovey and Lynn McNair take us on a journey which emphasises different aspects of the Froebelian approach in updated forms relevant to today.

At a roughly half way point in the book, Jane Read guides the reader full circle to practice in the UK when at the beginning of the 20th century, when Froebel's influence began to take root. The importance of keeping the Froebelian principles, and not outdated practice, which soon becomes too prescribed and outmoded, cannot be emphasised too much.

Maureen Baker, Jenny Spratt and Marjorie Ouvry focus on the importance of the arts in a child's education in the context of today, with music and rhyme in the Froebelian tradition. Home learning in the family is an important part of this.

The importance of creating environments conducive to learning is given attention in the chapter by Jane Whinnett, who examines the contribution of wooden blockplay (the Gifts) and three and two dimensional arts (the Occupations). These are as important now as they were in Froebel's time. Chris McCormick sets out the place of cookery in Froebelian practice today, giving a detailed account of one of the Occupations in current contexts.

The authors have emphasised the practical aspects of the work, whilst identifying the Froebelian principles which serve as navigational tools. In this way, the practice is constantly reflected upon, modified, adapted, transformed or reaffirmed, while the principles remain, acting as a resource for each generation to explore and reassert in ways that are right for a particular historic time, diverse cultures, communities and families.

The importance of warmth and affection in childhood

Friedrich Froebel was born 21 April, 1782 in the German village of Oberwissbach in the Thuringian Forest. He was the youngest of six children, and when he was nearly a year old, his mother died. His father, a stern and rigid thinking pastor married his second wife a year later. Until she had her own baby, she enjoyed her stepson's company, but then she rejected him.

He spent a lonely childhood in the garden of the vicarage, which was surrounded by a high wall. This gave him his life-long fascination with nature and its laws, and equipped him for his later studies at University. When he reached early adolescence (1793) he went to live with his mother's brother, a gentler pastor, who saw how hard Froebel's childhood was, and he was apprenticed informally to learn about forestry. At University in Jena his diary shows his search for order, the interconnectivity of things, and unity within a world of diversity in which each child and adult is unique as well as part of humanity. His study of plants, trees and animals continued to fascinate him, together with mathematics.

After a brief time at home helping in his father's parish until the latter's death in 1802, with reconciliation between father and son, and more contact with his older brothers and sisters, especially Christoph, he worked on farms for little payment until he went to Frankfurt. This city was in a state of rapid change from deep conservatism to more liberal ways of thinking. He worked in a school based on

Pestalozzi's ideas. He made two visits to Pestalozzi's school in Yverdun in Switzerland, financed by Caroline von Holzhausen, for whose children he was tutor.

Teamwork is important

He met Christian Langethal and Wilhelm Middendorff whilst serving in the Napoleonic Wars in 1813. They became lifelong companions and taught in his schools. The first school, in Keihau (1817) was attended by the orphaned sons of his brother Christoph. In 1818 he married Wilhelmine Hoffmeister. Langethal, Middendorff, Wilhelmine and a younger teacher, Barop, contributed in deep ways to the development of Froebelian education.

The kindergarten

In 1840 Froebel's invention, the kindergarten (garden of children) was established in Blankenburg (Weston, 2002). This showed his determination to highlight the importance of the child's development and education in the first years of life. The publication of the Mother Songs in 1844 further emphasised this.

Froebel's belief that women are capable of becoming teachers

Liebschner (1992: 29) reports that in 'An Appeal to German Women' (1848) he wrote:

> ... if we men work separately, unaided by you and your sex in some permanent and effective manner, we cannot, with all our efforts, accomplish anything comprehensive and satisfactory, either for separate families, still less for the nation, least of all for mankind at large, though the need is everywhere pressing.

It is an ironic twist that the situation is now reversed, with few men becoming early childhood practitioners in most countries of the world.

In 1849 a training course was set up in Liebenstein.

In 1850 his kindergartens in Prussia were closed when the 'Kindergarten Verbot' was issued by the King, but this had the opposite effect to the one intended. Many Froebel teachers went abroad to work, carrying with them the Froebelian approach to education. Froebel died in 1852, having married the kindergarten teacher, Louise Levin, the year before.

In this book, important aspects of his work are reflected upon. His work remains a resource from which current practitioners draw useful thoughts which are transformed into this day and age, and which have flexibility to be used in diverse cultural contexts.

Family and community are of central importance, together with the way these aspects of his work link to the wider world and universe. This is not a fragmented view of education. The cliché of the whole child is re-examined with this in mind.

Froebel's journey into becoming an educational pioneer began with the time he spent as a young child in the garden. It is appropriate that there is great emphasis in this book on the learning that is deep and meaningful and lasting throughout life which takes place in the outdoor context.

Reflective Question

- In some countries of the world trained practitioners, and especially teachers, are expected to be able to locate their practice in terms of the philosophical influences which impact on how they practice. Can you?

Introductory reading

Bruce, T., Meggitt, C. and Grenier, J. (2010) *Child Care and Education*, 5th edn. London: Hodder Education.

Bruce, T. (2011a) *Early Childhood Education*, 4th edn. London: Hodder Education.

Weston, P. (2002) *The Froebel Educational Institute: The Orgins and History of the College*. Roehampton: University of Surrey.

Further reading

Liebschner, J. (1992) *A Child's Work: Freedom and Guidance in Froebel's Educational Theory and Practice*. Cambridge: Lutterworth Press.

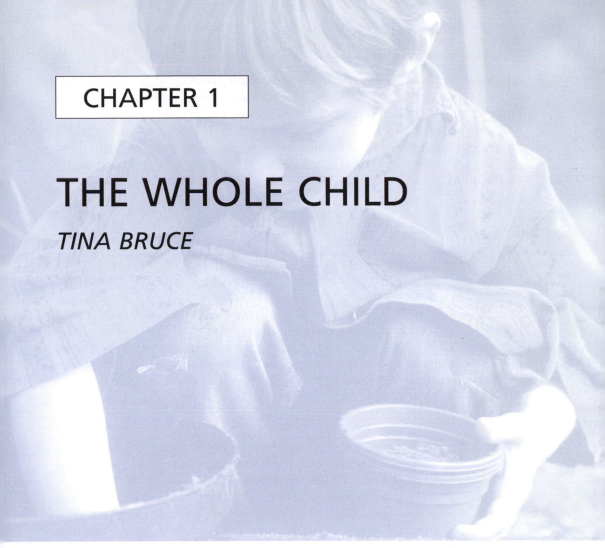

CHAPTER 1

THE WHOLE CHILD

TINA BRUCE

The whole child – the child's relationship with self, others and the universe

At regular intervals in the history of the world, there are clashes between people who hold different views of the world. Sometimes a way of thinking will creep quietly and gently into people's minds, difficult to put into words, almost a group feeling that this is how things are or ought to be. At other times there is a clarion call for change, and old moth-eaten ideas are ruthlessly attacked and put on the rubbish dump. This is as true for theoretical frameworks as it is for political systems and governments.

The Froebelian framework that is put forward in this book is not a new one. It started life in the middle of the nineteenth century – the period of the Enlightenment. But it still has a time-honoured place in early childhood education and care. This is because a good framework transforms itself and is as relevant today as it was when it was first formed. The principles and philosophy of Friedrich Froebel have lasting value and have become a navigational tool, leading reflective practitioners in different parts of the world into a new era. In this way, something which started as a small idea has rippled out into something larger and of lasting value.This is well expressed in a saying on the notice board outside a Quaker Meeting House in Hammersmith recently:

> I set my hope on the small inner circles which ripple outwards and in doing so transform and grow, changing self and others.

The Enlightenment, which certainly influenced the original thinking of Friedrich Froebel (1782–1852), has at its heart several key features. These are that:

- people need to be educated to think for themselves and not to rely on the thinking of others in authority to tell them what they should think
- there should be tolerance such that we can put our ideas into the public domain without fear of retribution from political, religious or other such authorities that have power to punish those whose ideas they disapprove of
- the past is seen as a resource to inform and transform the present and the future.

These ideas are strongly represented in this book which is about how Froebelian practice is being developed today in the UK. Froebel was influenced by the German Enlightenment philosopher, Immanuel Kant (1724–1804). But it is also important to remember that the Scottish Enlightenment was responsible for a surge forward in thinking which had particular features. These are also central in this book. Broadie (2007) is of the view that the Scottish Enlightenment uniquely involved a close-knit community of thinkers who shared, debated and reflected on ideas together, such as the two friends, David Hume and Adam Smith.

The group who initiated this book are in that mould. The Froebel network in Edinburgh comes from a long and respected tradition, which has allowed depth of discussions, some of which have been, and will continue to be, robust and challenging. Feeling safe enough to explore and critically reflect (through being linked into a Froebel network of this kind) has led to the practitioners feeling able to discuss regularly the educational principles of Friedrich Froebel, and to study them with rigour through short one-day courses and an accredited Froebel course at the University of Edinburgh. This kind of close-knit community is important, but contact with the wider world of education is also important. Just as the literati groups which were such a feature of the Scottish Enlightenment linked with commerce, science, and ecclesiastical life, so the Edinburgh Froebel network is strongly linked with educational ideas beyond. This provides opportunities to put in the public domain (such as this book and conferences) the reflections on Froebelian principles that have developed, leading to consideration of what Froebelian practice might look like, and how it transforms (without losing its essence) to take in the rich cultural diversity across the world.

Central to Froebel's thinking is the idea that education is about the relationship between self, others and the universe. These elements make up a whole and lead to an understanding and respect for the unity that is in all things. Nowadays we no longer describe this as 'unity'. Instead, we usually talk about the whole child.

The whole child – what does it mean?

This term has become a cliché. It means different things to different people, but in this book it is developed to have meaning for Froebelians today. It involves an updating of terminology which ensures that the concept of unity remains, but as a navigational tool that has use, application and meaning today.

In developing this concept of the 'whole' (unity), Froebel brought together many existing ideas. In doing so, across the years, slowly and gradually, by the time he died in 1852, he had developed an understanding of the need to see children as whole people with thoughts, feelings, physical selves, and relationships to others. He placed the child in context, not in isolation from others or the universe. He did this in a larger way than those before him, but he used the past and others more contemporary to inform his approach. This thinking about the whole child continues to inform practitioners today, but it needs to be transformed into the context of today and the cultural setting in which it is to be used. Just as there are no two children who are the same (although they all have physical selves, intellectual lives, feelings and relationships) in the same way there are no two settings or classrooms the same (although they might have Froebelians practising in them). Froebelian practice embraces diversity, held together by elements which make it whole (giving it unity).

Like Kant, Froebel believed that we experience life through the senses and movements, through which we have sensory and kinaesthetic feedback. Also like Kant, he believed that we have the possibility to transform these experiences and to develop, in doing this, the symbolic. The symbolic life developed by the child is, in Froebel's view, a crucial part of being human. Experience which is real and direct with materials, nature and people is the bedrock of this, and childhood play is another central part of its development.

Learning by active participation and making connections

Most educators today would agree that children learn by doing and active participation and initiation in their lives, but Froebel's insistence on the wholeness of that experience is still not understood or embedded. Children might study trees, or grow plants in the garden, but for Froebel this needs to connect with the whole. There must be wholeness and unity of experience, which makes the meaning great for the learning child or adult. Trees take soil and air and they also give to the air and the soil. They contribute to the way the climate functions in different parts of the world. Children might watch fish in an aquarium, but they need to see a river and learn which fish live there and how. They need to understand about freshwater fish and sea fish. They need to see the sea to fully understand this. They need to know about running water environments and still water ponds. It is surprising how much children can learn and understand about nature study in the first seven years of their lives. This wholeness of learning is the kind that will stay with them for the rest of their lives. Each aspect of the experience links to another, opening up deeper understanding of the whole. Froebel stresses the importance of interconnected experiences. The result is a whole (unified) experience.

In the same way, if learning about fruit and vegetables is to have meaning, logic, coherence and to be a whole understanding, it will need to be about more than presenting children with plastic fruit. An apple, for example, grows on a tree. Children need to experience this. Some schools now plant orchards, but this is not yet widespread, or considered to be part of basic learning. Apple trees rely on bees to cross-pollinate. They need the right climate (temperature, sun, rain). Learning about different apples and what they are for (cooking, eating) and then learning to apply this with recipes, or sharing fruit to eat makes the study of apples fascinating, deep and meaningful for children.

Sharing fruit together brings a different wholeness to the child's development and learning. The relationship with self will bring the child to understand which fruits are favourite, how to eat them, cut them up, enjoy the experience. But it will also connect the child with others. If several children want the one banana what happens then? There can be discussion of whether it could be cut or broken into pieces. The child who has visited botanical gardens and seen bunches of bananas grow, or visited countries where they grow naturally, will quickly become aware of the temperature and climate bananas need in order to grow. This connects the child with the wider universe. So does making compost with the skin, and turning it to soil. Would this help the apple tree to grow?

Through these examples, which show just a few of the possibilities through which children learn to be whole people, the importance of unity of experience which is inter-connected is clear. So often the learning experiences offered to children lack these important elements, and so the learning is far less than it could be. This is a waste of childhood, which is when most learning, (and certainly the foundations of the dispositions which encourage it), takes place. In the chapters which follow, the practical impact of the need for wholeness of first-hand, direct experience will be ever present and central.

The child as a symbol user and maker

A symbol is something which stands for and represents something else. Once a child is free from being rooted in the present, and can go back and forward in time, the symbolic life takes off. Walking, talking and pretending all seem to come together. Pretending and talking is part of having a symbolic life.

In the last section several of the examples given feature Froebel's emphasis on the importance of the study of and relationship with nature as part of the basic education of a child. Song, rhyme, stories are also interconnecting and whole experiences with literature, music which involve children in symbolic ways. These also connect children with self, others, and the universe. We see this in the Movement Games and the Mother Songs. Because cultures develop or vary, through different historic times, or in different parts of the world, these are no longer used in the way they were originally. But the essential messages remain.

Children learn best when they can use what they know and understand to learn about what is new to them. They use what they know as a jumping-off point, equipped with dealing with what is not familiar to them. For example, once you know that apples grow on trees, it is possible to understand that oranges do too. You do not have to grow an orange tree to be able to understand quite a bit about how that happens. The important thing, as Froebel realised, is that children are not required to learn what is beyond biological maturity.

Developing the symbolic life of the child through music, song and rhyme

The same approach is used in the choice of songs, music, rhymes and stories selected by Froebelian practitioners today. The subjects for songs, movement games (finger and action songs) and stories that Froebel chose were based on everyday experiences, and the physical self-knowledge of children. These were about the baker, the dovecot, the charcoal burner, the carpenter, for example. Now children sing about buses, cars, aeroplanes, doctors, buying buns. But they do not focus on these in respecting the work being done, or understanding the processes of baking the buns. Froebel's respect for craft and work essential for everyday life and communities perhaps needs reactivation.

Typically the songs sung to and with children are rather superficial in their content, and in the melodies and rhythms. Perhaps this is because few practitioners in the UK today can sight-read any more, or play by ear. Before the days of records, CDs and DVDs, computers and other technologies bringing tunes and music into the home or early childhood setting ready-made, adults learned to sing from memory complex songs, or to play musical instruments by ear, and, in some circles, to sight-read music. The words of songs, the complexity of illustrations in songbooks with layers of symbolic meaning, all need attention in the musical and movement aspects of early childhood education. Children are being underestimated in this respect because the adults they spend time with are not equipped to help them develop as much as they could, if given the opportunities. They are also functioning at lower levels in relation to the sophistication of the melody and rhythms, or the movements that are part of the music and movement experience.

Children need to spend time with adults whose minds have been expanded through music and dance, three-and two-dimensional visual arts, literature and drama, as central to this. Children depend on adults to teach them about these through participation in their culture. Depending on the adults they spend time with, they will either have less-than-whole or whole experiences. They will either live whole, fulfilled artistic lives, or not. This is the difference between a broad, rich and deep education, and narrow schooling.

The cultural aspect of educating children is a crucial strand, but so is the biological. Songs and dances and action songs and finger rhymes, used and developed in the Froebelian tradition build on what the child naturally does. Examples are walking, jumping, hopping, skipping, sliding and running.

Developing the symbolic life of the child through movement and dance

The symbolic life burgeons as children begin to walk, talk and pretend. You can walk round a chair, but you can only walk parallel to a wall. Toddlers love these kinds of movement games, and adults, family or practitioners can spend happy times together making up songs to accompany this, all about straight lines and round and round.

Froebel developed 'wandering games' and 'visiting games'. These involved meeting people in a particular order, greetings of characters, invitations and events (imagined and real). The dances were designed for children who had developed enough experience and biological maturity (typically 5–8 years of age) to form figures of eight, and other shapes. There were representations of, for example, a snail. This made a spiral shape, echoing nature. Other movements showed a woodland, swimming, birds flying, tying a bow, planting seeds, working in the garden, feeding chickens and a cat playing with a mouse.

The mill wheel involved children in dancing formed of two concentric circles, with the outer circle moving faster than the inner circle. This gave tangible form to a scientific concept in the working of machinery and technology. Games suitable for the culture and everyday lives of children growing up today in different parts of the world need to be developed in the Froebelian traditions.

Knowledge, everyday life and beauty and how they connect with each other

All of these artistic experiences developed the whole child through the ideas and imagination, physical body and the emotional mind. Froebel believed that these were all interconnected as a coherent and integrated whole. He called them the forms of knowledge, life and beauty, respectively. Everything, in his view, is interconnected. He talked about the need to link, and link as central to being educated.

According to Froebel, symbols hold meanings which grow out of active life, and which translate actions back to the inner meaning of life. It is not enough to observe and describe or represent a garden with plants growing in it. It is essential to act on what is seen and described, through digging, sowing seeds, planting bulbs, and looking after the plants and insect life.

The same applies in the social life of the home or early childhood setting. Both adults and children learn through each other as they play and work together. Often educators say that children learn with other children, but Froebel emphasised the way that children and adults learn through each other.

Through their own actions, children manipulate objects, learn through people, represent experiences symbolically. All of this is important, but Froebel's important contribution is to show the importance of the child's autonomy and intrinsic motivation in this. He calls it the self-activity of the child. The child is learning to think for him or herself, to know how to get the help needed when needed, to willingly accept being taught directly when it makes sense.

The Gifts and Occupations

Froebel was the first educationalist to place wooden blocks at the heart of a child's education. He saw play with these had the potential to teach children mathematics, language, about beauty and artistic endeavours, scientific construction, stories, the representation of everyday life and to be physically competent and skilled. In the 1830s he stressed the importance of children using these blocks in their free play, with adults supporting and joining in appropriately (Liebschner, 1992). He became more prescriptive in 1844, but Liebschner suggests that as he saw practitioners invade and take over the children's learning, he moved again to a less adult-dominated approach.

The degree to which adults lead children in their play remains an area of contention for the practitioners and parents of today. It seems that it is fine for adults to join children in their play providing they are sensitive to children's ideas. After all, the aim is to develop the child's learning, and not so much the learning of the adult! Adults need to build their own constructions alongside the child, rather than take over that of the child. In order to educate rather than school and instruct children in narrow ways, practitioners need to be good and informed observers. They need to know about child development which they use as a navigational tool. They also need to have played with blocks themselves, so that they know the potential of the material. (The same applies to clay, sand, water or any other material offered to children.) They need to have studied the mathematical, scientific and dramatic opportunities too. The Tickell Review (2011) of the English Early Years Framework strongly states the importance, when working with other people's children, of educated, mature, well-trained and qualified practitioners.

The Gifts – wooden blockplay

The first Gift is the soft sphere. The second is the wooden sphere, cube and cylinder, suspended on string. This demonstrates the law of opposites. What is known is challenged by experience, and new connections with what is known before need to be made. Nowadays the first and second Gifts are virtually never seen, and only the Froebelian principle behind them remains, although babies are still often and typically given the soft sphere as a first Gift. Most people do not realise that this is a link to Froebel's educational approach.

These first and second Gifts can be rotated and spun such that they transform into different shapes. It is significant that the wooden blocks (Gifts 3 to 5) were presented to children in a whole box with a sliding lid, which was slid from underneath leaving a cube made up of smaller cubes. The parts make the whole – a central Froebelian message. Each box of the Gifts contained small blocks of different shapes, carefully thought through. These are not used in their original form today. Froebel was a mathematician by training, and a forester, and it is these aspects which make wooden blockplay particularly important in a child's education. The modern form of Froebel's Gifts can be found in those known as Unit blocks, Hollow blocks, mini-unit and mini-hollow blocks. There is a direct link through Community Playthings with Froebel's first school in Keihau (Huleatt, 2011). Each block, in the Froebelian tradition, links with others. The natural wood links the child to nature, and this connection to trees needs to be made explicit. The child needs to see the maple tree (or, if it is an old set of blocks, the beech tree) from which the blocks are made in order to have a whole experience.

The Occupations – workshop experiences

The Occupations are the sorts of things that would be found in workshop areas of early childhood settings. In today's context they include drawing, painting, clay, paper-folding and junk-modelling, cutting, pattern-making with shape boards and tessellations, printing and paper-pricking, weaving, sewing and construction kits. But they are offered separately and in a fragmented way. The unity and interconnectedness between them has become lost, and needs to be re-established in ways which are right for diverse communities in different parts of the world today. Each Occupation offers children different challenges, and children learn to generate their own problems and to solve them, to be imaginative and creative, physically and mindfully skilled. The Occupations need to be made a whole experience again, if they are to make their full contribution to the learning of children.

Play

Froebel (anticipating Vygotsky, 1978) saw play as the highest form of learning. This was because it orchestrates learning into a whole. Nowadays it is seen as an integrating mechanism. Drawing on the wealth of research and theories of play, 12 features emerge (Bruce, 1991, updated 2011b) which resonate with the Froebelian traditions in updated form. When these co-ordinate the play develops a free-flowing character, and so the 12 features identified as central to play are named 'free flow play' (Bruce, 1991, updated 2011b).

1   Children draw upon the first-hand experiences they have had. They bring these into their play. The richer their experiences of ideas, thoughts, feelings, relationships and their physical bodies, the richer the play can be.
2   Play shows us what children understand about rules of different kinds. These will be social greetings and partings, organisational, fairness, singing games, stories, mathematics and many others kinds of rules. When they play children are in control, and they make their own rules.
3   Children find props, or make them when they play. They get the idea that this is possible from seeing other people play. Making dens, pretending leaves are plates and twigs are cutlery or chopsticks are open-ended props, which lend themselves to the development of imagination and creativity through play.
4   Play cannot be forced upon children. A child has to be in the right frame of mind and mood to play. Children choose to play or not. Play will not fit into tight timetables. Children need time and space and people who encourage play in order for it to flourish and develop with depth. Play needs the right circumstances, conditions and atmosphere. Then it burgeons.
5   In their play, children escape from the here and now. They can transform the past, and shape the future to their liking, experiment with situations, rearrange, reflect, create alternatives, feel stronger and equipped to make things better in future, dealing with things differently. They can recapture past pleasures, reassure, enjoy. Children manage pain and come to terms with life in their play. They find what they value most. They hold on to what they treasure in their play. They become more resilient (Brown, 2004).

6 Children pretend when they play, moving from the literal to the more abstract, from being like other people, to being in the character or the story they make up.

7 Froebel stressed that education involves children in better knowing themselves, others and the universe. Playing alone is part of this. There is a difference between being lonely and feeling alone and getting to know self through having the personal space that encourages this. Many children and adults today do not have enough personal space, and this makes reflection and thoughtful action difficult.

8 Children often mirror and imitate each other as they play. They may enjoy each other's companionship without wishing to directly interact and engage with each other.

9 Children who develop their play with great depth will vary the nature of their play, sometimes playing alone, sometimes in parallel companionship and sometimes co-operatively. When children play co-operatively they need to be clear about the theme and who is being who. Each child will develop their own play agenda and follow it, while needing to be sensitive to the needs, thoughts and feelings of fellow players. The recognition that they are part of a whole play episode develops. Some adults have not yet developed this ability, as seen when they invade and take over the play, rather than joining in with the understanding that their play agenda is no more important than that of anyone else participating in the play.

10 Children who play well are deeply involved in their play. They are not distracted in their concentration and focused learning by events or others. Being engaged in learning is one of the hallmarks and predictors of successful future learning in the school system. Childhood play is an appropriate form through which concentration develops.

11 Children who are involved in their play are able to apply their learning. The application of knowledge is key to sound education. Development and learning come together, resulting in technical competence and skills. It is not so much that children learn new things in their play. It is more that they try out what they have been learning and thinking, feeling and physically doing when they play. Play is a powerful tool through which to observe the learning children have been developing, and to see its impact in a child-safe environment.

12 Play takes children to their highest forms of learning, revealing the future inner life. It is a resource which remains deep inside the maturing child, encouraging adult creativity, problem-solving and imagination, and dispositions conducive to the development of future learning. It is an integrating mechanism which makes learning whole and not compartmentalised and fragmented.

It is important that those who spend time with other people's children throughout their professional lives continue to study and observe play.

Froebel's thinking about play was born out of practice. The more he played with children, the more he learned from them. Then he had to modify, change and update his ideas about play, which he continued to do throughout his life. The situation is no different for practitioners today.

Froebel (1782–1852) took the natural play of children and gave it educational status. His pioneering work spread across Europe and into the USA. Later, Rudolf Steiner (1861–1925) also gave status to play, again using open-ended, natural materials (Taplin, 2010). The central place given to childhood play by Froebel, and subsequently Steiner, contrasts with the approach of Maria Montessori (1869–1952). She felt that children need to engage in real rather play experience, such as pretend cooking. Montessorians today (Montessori Schools Association, 2008) continue to emphasise as defining factors in the child's education having freedom of choice, and the exercise of will and deep engagement, leading to concentration. Freedom of choice is, however, limited to the exercises and experiences of the 'prepared environment' to which the child has been introduced by the trained Montessorian. This is a great contrast to the practice of Froebelians and Steinerians who place play as well as rich first hand experiences at the centre of education. Steinerians are doubtful of the early introduction of technology, such as camera, books, and computers or word processors, mobile phones etc. Froebelians see children as part of their community from the beginning of life, and technology is a part of the lives of children today, to which children take easily and with joy. Through play, children transform, vary, abstract, develop, imagine, create and innovate as they move into the future. Play lifts children to higher levels of functioning than everyday experiences which are literal and in the here and now. Play helps children to transform their learning and take it from the immediate here and now, to the past and future, and to use their experience as a resource, going beyond the real world as increasingly skilled symbol users and symbol makers.

The whole child – including the family and the community

From the Gifts and Occupations, Nature, Movement Games, Mother Songs (with finger rhymes and action songs) and emphasis on play, Froebel developed a whole, unified approach to the education of young children. This had inner logic and cohesion which did not prescribe or constrain the self-activity of the child. Autonomous learning was encouraged, and the child's intrinsic motivation supported by adults, sensitive to what is needed through observation and understanding of child development integrated with thorough knowledge and understanding of the core curriculum areas of experience. For Froebel these were helping children to understand time, space, reasons for things, nature, mathematics, literature and the arts, movement and the physical self-such that they were educated in relating to self, others and the universe through the forms of knowledge (intellectual life) everyday life (physically participating) and beauty (emotional life of feelings and relationships). Then the child would be a whole person.

There is another aspect of the notion of the whole child which has permeated this chapter, but needs more articulation, and that is the way that family and community are at the heart of education. The child is not separate from other people, in the home or in the community and wider world. This is the focus of the next chapter.

Reflective questions and practical actions

Observe a child or children at play. Using the features outlined, reflect on whether the play is of deep quality.

- In your setting, do you consider that you offer first-hand experiences to children, which are interconnected and whole? Can you make changes which would do so with more impact on the learning taking place?

Introductory reading

Bruce, T. (2011b) *Learning through Play*. 2nd edn. London: Hodder Education.
Community Playthings (2008) *I Made a Unicorn! Open-ended Play with Blocks and Simple Materials*. Robertsbridge, E. Sussex: Community Playthings.

Further reading

Bruce, T. (2011a) *Early Childhood Education*. 4th edn. London: Hodder Arnold.
Bruce, T. (2001d) *Cultivating Creativity: Babies, Toddlers and Young Children*. 2nd edn. London: Hodder Education.
Liebschner, J. (1992) *A Child's Work: Freedom and Guidance in Froebel's Educational Theory and Practice*. Cambridge: Lutterworth Press.
Whinnett, J. (2006) 'Froebelian practice today: the search for unity', *Early Childhood Practice: The Journal for Multi-Professional Partnerships*, 8(2): 58–80.

CHAPTER 2

FAMILY, COMMUNITY AND THE WIDER WORLD

TINA BRUCE

Family

It is important to remember the cultural context and historic time in which Froebel was developing his work on the education of young children. His thinking about family life will therefore not be identical with thinking today. However, as always when exploring his thoughts, there are key principles which are as important today as they were then. It is equally important to bear in mind that the contexts of today are different, and will change as thinking develops about the relationships between children and their families. Families are no longer seen as a standard entity. Instead, they are considered to be varied and diverse. Patterns of family organisation and structure differ in different parts of the world, and also within communities and countries. No two families are the same, or have ever been the same.

Froebel seemed to recognise this intuitively. He did not tell parents how to bring up their children, but he did believe that parents will have too daunting a task if they have to bring up their children isolated from their community. He would probably have agreed with the African proverb which says that it takes a whole village to bring up a child. Parents, in his view, need encouragement and support. They need to be empowered.

We can see that there are two key principles to be taken from Froebel's approach to working with parents. The first is that professionally trained practitioners should respect parents and the families they work with. The second is that parenting is a lonely and anxious endeavour unless there is a supportive community which the family is a part of.

Two very different ways of working with families

Currently there are two strands in the way that practitioners work with parents. One is a deficit approach. The other builds on strengths and empowers parents. In this book the traditional Froebelian approach is taken, and so schools and early childhood settings are seen as part of the community, together with parents and children.

People are not taught how to be parents. They are respected and encouraged to be part of a learning community, in close partnership with practitioners who are learning as much as the parents are about the best and most fulfilling ways of helping young children to develop, learn and flourish. A third Froebelian principle emerges here. Professionals and parents work together, each offering what they know and understand about the children. The parent lives with their child, and so knows them best. The professional knows about children and how they develop and learn in general, but needs help in tuning into the particular child, helped to do so through working with the parent in a close and respectful partnership. The professional needs to know about child development and also about the areas and content of knowledge and understanding which the community, society and wider world have identified as important.

However, a strong and important principle part of the Froebelian approach is to identify (through observation), support and help the child to extend their interests and what fascinates them in educationally worthwhile directions.

Realisation that the earliest years are crucial for developing learning

We now know that the first years of life are the important years in encouraging dispositions towards learning which will go with children through their lives, providing they are not damaged through later bad experiences of narrow, meaningless learning. During Froebel's life there was a slow dawning of realisation that the care of young children is important, and could be a life and death matter. Rousseau had caused a revolution in childcare by encouraging mothers to breastfed their babies, rather than giving them to a wet nurse. Jane Austen's mother was typical in this. Her children were breastfed until they became mobile, and then they lived with foster parents in the village until they could walk, talk and were toilet-trained, when they returned home.

Typically, children were seen as miniature adults, wearing adult clothes, until Rousseau challenged this and caused debate which resulted in change. Clothes giving freedom of movement became acceptable for everyday life during Froebel's life.

Children were at the heart of the family, joining social occasions and events. But while the physical needs of children were becoming better understood and parents were becoming more informed in relation to these, the emotional and intellectual lives of children were often neglected. This was not because children were wittingly abused. This was for the simple reason that adults were usually unaware of these concepts, or did not realise they were important in childhood. In other words, the emphasis was on the physical care of children, which was considered important in ensuring that children were physically strong and healthy, and well behaved.

Froebel introduced and advocated the importance of education for young children. He realised that children are fulfilled in their developing learning if they find it interesting and can be active participants. He realised, as we saw in Chapter 1, that this involves the whole child, physically, but also their thoughts, ideas, feelings and relationships. Education is a bigger concept than care. It involves the whole child. Often nowadays the term childcare is used, or childcare and education. This is because the child is still not seen as the whole child. There is still the tendency to fragment and separate off different aspects of the child.

The medical profession focuses on physical care and the therapies emphasise, mental health. Day-care workers in the private, voluntary and independent sectors together with childminders have traditionally emphasised care, which has included the social, emotional and physical care of the child. Froebel believed that the intellectual life of the child is also important, and is present from the beginning of life until the day we die. He saw education as a birth to death process, with every stage being important, but the early years having the potential to get children off to a good start in all aspects. Education is a concept which embraces the intellectual life as well as other areas of development and learning. A rich intellectual life brings with it fulfilment, which is deeply linked to well-being, self-confidence, high self-esteem and the ability to relate well to others, as well as knowing yourself and how to manage yourself.

The importance of having warm, loving relationships

For Froebel, the mother who spends time with her children is a key person in their early education, but he does include fathers and grandparents and brothers and sisters too. Nowadays fathers and grandparents are much more involved in the upbringing of children in many families. The family is at the heart of the educational process in the Froebelian tradition.

When we consider the lives of some of the great pioneers who have contributed much in making better the lives of young children, it is remarkable how many of them experienced difficult and challenging early lives. This situation can go two ways.

Some react by asserting that they had a terrible time and survived, and that we should not be romantic about children. They argue that children are tough and resilient and that what is needed more than anything else is to give them the keys to release them from a bad childhood into a successful adult life. For some this means putting them to work early. For others it means a forceful introduction to the 3 Rs which, it is thought, is their passport to a better future. A substantial minority of politicians and commercial entrepreneurs fall into this category.

Others, such as John Bowlby (Holmes, 1993) or Margaret McMillan (Bradburn, 1989) or Froebel react in a different way. They do not want other children to suffer as they have done. They want to improve family life, or the schools and early childhood settings that children spend time in. Children need some stability in relationships, which should not be ever-changing. In their view, more than anything else, children need to be loved and cherished through at least one close and loving relationship (Bruce, 2011c; Elfer and Grenier, 2010; Gerhardt, 2007). This ensures that they are sufficiently at ease with themselves and can manage themselves so that they relate well to self and others.

But this is not enough. The nurturing of children's interests is one strand which brings, in very meaningful ways, a rich intellectual life, full of satisfaction and energising and harnessing the natural motivation that is intrinsic in babies and toddlers, and protecting this from damage as children grow up. But as well as fulfilling the needs of the emerging strong self, Froebel also reminds us that children are interconnected with their families, and through them communities and the wider world. This is where the professional practitioner becomes important in supporting and empowering families. Families do not function in isolation from the rest of society. They are part of it. Froebel found that parents deeply appreciated practitioners who became a bridge between the family and the community and wider world. Parents know their children and spend time with them, working on intuition. Intuition is about experienced hunches. It is a deep kind of knowledge and understanding. Parents do not have experience when their first child is born, but they usually become more confident when subsequent children are born.

Working with parents in a close partnership

Parents do not need to be told what to do. But they appreciate professionals who know about child development, and who use this to help parents by articulating what they intuitively know. Intuition does not need or use words. It is fine to operate at an intuitive level within the family, because there is little need to talk about how children are being brought up. There are unspoken understandings. But professionals, working with other people's children, do need to be articulate about the knowledge they possess. They also need a deep knowledge of how children develop and learn, and the environments, both peopled and material, which make them flourish. Observation, child development, curriculum, pedagogy and subject knowledge are all necessary and important parts of the expertise of professional practitioners.

Unless practitioners can apply the knowledge they have, they tend to fall back on telling parents what to do. Froebel was consistent in his way of working. He observed first, and it was out of practice that theory developed. He was a mathematician and a forester by training and apprenticeship respectively. He was also a crystallographer. Observation was central to this field, as it has always been in the history of science (Rowland, 2011). His way of working helps parents to get to grips with what is useful and important knowledge and understanding to develop in their children. Seeing a cow milked, watching the milk treated and sent to the shop, and buying a bottle or carton of milk teaches children more than being given milk to drink each day. Walking down the street, watching the roadsweeper and visiting the refuse dump helps children to learn about the way the community is structured and organised. Froebel respected every worker for their contribution, and taught children to do so too. This helps parents to choose books and DVDs which are educational, rather than just fun and occupying.

Community schools

Froebel developed the concept of the community school, with an open-door approach which welcomed parents joining in. There was group dancing and singing, and events were celebrated together as a community. In the village of Blankenburg there is now a museum honouring his work. It is situated in the first kindergarten he opened. In the village there is a fountain in the square where he took the children to dance and sing, and they visited the shopkeepers. The kindergarten was in the heart of the community.

Of course, not all children have a family at the centre of their lives, and Froebel was all too aware of this. His mother had died when he was a toddler, and he spent a lonely childhood, much of it in the garden alone. His father was a cold and stern Lutheran pastor. He married again and, until Froebel's stepmother had her own child, she made a great fuss of Friedrich, but after she became a mother she rejected him. Froebel knew a great deal about loss and lack of warm affection and love in early childhood. He later went to live with his uncle and his mother's sister, in early adolescence. His uncle was a gentler Lutheran pastor, and here he continued his interest in forests and nature in a warmer and kinder atmosphere. It is perhaps significant that he later adopted into his first school in Keilhau his orphaned nephews. This was a boarding school and a day school but he tried to create a sense of a caring community from the beginning of his work.

Behaviour

Behaviour and how children should be disciplined has always been a concern of parents and teachers alike. It can quickly become the priority which detracts from the main purpose of a school and takes over family life. It rapidly takes staff and parents into an approach which places the child's deficits at the centre, rather than taking a view that families and schools should build on the strengths of children. Froebel took the view, which arose as did his entire approach, that behind every bit of bad behaviour, there is a good intention. He saw the role of the parent or professional practitioner as identifying the good intention, and then working with that. This means that in his approach there will need to be plenty of discussion about how unsatisfactory and unacceptable situations have emerged, and what went wrong. Children participate in establishing what needs to be done in future to avoid situations, and what would help them to try to put things right or, failing that, to make amendments. In this way, children are not judged. Firm, clear boundaries are explained and made clear. Boundaries are adjusted, or new ones made. Children are encouraged to help each other, rather than to compete. This is a learning community, where each helps and supports the other, and where children and adults feel safe and secure with firm, clear boundaries. Only then will children and adults be free to explore, to be creative and enjoy each other's company as they do so. This is what Froebel called freedom with guidance (Liebschner, 1992).

Even today the Froebelian approach survives, but the climate is hostile to this approach to behaviour management. Star charts prevail, setting children in competition with each other, and with adults extrinsically controlling behaviour. This is a far cry from Froebel's belief that education is about making the inner outer and the outer inner through the self-activity of the child. It certainly takes courage to act on the view that children are intrinsically trying to be good, in the sense that they have no inner desire to upset others, to be cruel to them or to break materials. The way that babies and toddlers are treated plays a crucial part in this, and so does the child's experiences at home and in the early childhood setting at school and beyond.

Babies and toddlers, young and older children and adolescents, and adults, in fact human beings, are experimenters and active learners. If they are left to cry, not talked to very much or at all, punished when they do not understand, shut away when they have a temper tantrum, hit by someone bigger and stronger than them just because they have done something to displease this person with huge power and authority, they will experiment with ways of dealing with all of this. There is a vast range of possibilities – none of them what we would hope to see, and those which prove successful for them (in the sense that they bring short-term survival) will become entrenched and permanent.

Developing self-discipline rather than controlling behaviour

Typical behaviour will be doing what the adult wants in order to get the reward but, once the reward is gained, not bothering any more and not really understanding the essence of the message being taught. Extrinsic reward certainly brings short-term results, but the child who is rewarded with a treat for reading out loud to their parent their homework book at 4 years of age is less likely to turn into a bookworm than the child whose parent reads a more sophisticated story to them at bedtime each evening, which hooks them on literature for ever (Goouch, 2007).

The class of children who have a class treat for behaving well at storytime are less likely to enjoy coming together around situations involving dancing, singing, making music or sharing poetry and stories in a group than those who are encouraged to tidy up efficiently and quickly so that there is more time for this. They are more inclined to join in with a care for others if they are not nagged and regimented, but helped to see that joining in leads to a deeper and more fulfilling experience. Pace and singing interesting songs, dancing interesting dances, telling fascinating stories and sharing meaningful rhymes are the key, not trying to get children to pay attention superficially. Education is not about crowd control. It is about self-knowledge and participation in culture and community, and connecting to the wider world through other people and worthwhile experiences. Once this is at the centre of early childhood settings and families, self-discipline emerges rather than the adult management of a child's or group of children's behaviour. But the atmosphere must be conducive to bringing this about. This ethos is at the heart of the Froebelian family and community and the school or early childhood setting is an important part of it.

Froebel believed that education is about making the inner outer and the outer inner. In this respect his work resonates with the meaning of the word, education. Education comes from the verb *educare*, 'to lead out'. So often we hear education referred to as a putting in, with children regarded as empty vessels to be filled with what adults think is important for them to know. In the family context, children brought up in the Froebelian framework are offered what Froebel considered to be educationally worthwhile experiences, in which they participate actively. These begin with learning through the senses and the child's physical movements. They introduce nature, everyday life experiences, mathematical situations, the arts, including, music, song, three-dimensional and two-dimensional visual arts, literature, drama, movement and dance, and an introduction to time and space leading into history and geography, and an increasing understanding of the reasons for things which becomes scientific. (Froebel's interest in time, space and reasons was influenced by the philosophy of Immanuel Kant, who proposed this as the intellectual framework.) At the heart of Froebel's educational approach is relationship with self, others and the universe.

Family experiences which are rich

As the child begins to walk, talk and pretend, the parent supports the child as he or she moves into deeper, symbolic layers of meaning. This permeates every aspect of the child's home life, and ripples across into the early childhood setting. Parents who are supported in this process are in a position to enjoy their children's journey. Froebel emphasised the importance of parents and family living with and learning with their children. At the heart of this is a respect for children. Adults can learn as much from children as children learn from adults. Each can help the other. Parenthood brings out the child in the adult, and this can be a frightening aspect of parenthood, especially if the childhood was not a happy, secure or fulfilled one. But if helped to enjoy play and rich experiences with their children, being a parent becomes less daunting.

Many children nowadays, for a variety of reasons, do not spend much time out of doors either in the town, urban city or in the countryside. This does not only apply to the UK. Marjatta Kalliala (2004), a Froebelian trained in the Finnish context, writes about this. An urgent task for educators today is to make it easier for parents to take their children out. The pioneer work of Octavia Hill in establishing the 'Open Spaces Movement' in the urban areas of the UK at the turn of the nineteenth century saved land such as municipal parks and areas such as London Fields for large urban contexts. These remain places where families can go free of charge. The public-sector nursery schools have at their heart the garden as half the learning environment, with the indoor area as the other half. These were pioneered at the turn of the twentieth century by Froebelian Margaret McMillan. She recognised that, whereas middle-class children had gardens in which to play and learn through their homes, and were often educated in home-based kindergartens, children growing up in areas of urban poverty had no access to the outdoors except in the streets. Street play remained important for many children until the encroachment of the motor car and other motor transport in the streets, but in the nursery school children could play safely. Not only this, but in the nursery schools there were carefully planted gardens through which children learnt about nature. There was a tendency to preach at parents and to judge them, rather than to build on their strengths. This was a hallmark of the times, but the nursery schools nowadays (many if which have been transformed into integrated children's centres) have returned to their

Froebelian roots in embracing a more respectful approach to working with parents and families.

The Froebel Research Nursery School

Two examples in the 1970s and 1980s of the way in which Froebelian principles led to close partnership with parents in ways which still have impact on practice today, can be seen in the Froebel Research Nursery School Project and the Froebel Blockplay Collaborative Research Project.

In 1972 the Principal of the Froebel Educational Institute, Molly Brearley, initiated a free nursery school for children from an area where there was little provision and underprivilege prevailed. This was established in the grounds of the college. The Research Fellow appointed was Chris Athey. There were two central Froebelian themes in this project. One was the development of a close partnership with parents as part of a learning community of adults. In this community, the learning that staff and parents undertook together in observing and spending time with the children was shared.

The nursery followed the traditions of the Froebelian nursery school in the rich experiences offered, and the emphasis on giving children whole experiences. For example, tadpoles were collected from the college lake with the families, observed in a pond created in the nursery garden, and the frogs were then returned to the lake. There was discussion about the fact that frogs return instinctively to the lake or pond where they were spawned, and returning creatures to their habitat is an important aspect of the study of nature. Many parents had not seen frog spawn before, or tadpoles or frogs in a real-life context. They were as interested as the children, and the following year some requested a repeat of this experience. Books were lent for home use, and children were supported in representing their experiences through participation in music, dance, song, literature, drama, clay-modelling, junk-modelling and many other media.

The practitioners learnt how to support parents in helping their children to develop self-discipline. Most of the parents were anxious about taking their children to a lake, and one child did slip in, quickly retrieved with only wet feet. It was clear that the children were reluctant to hold their parent's hand when asked by the parent to do this. They had no understanding of why they must do so. The practitioners found that by asking the children to hold their parent's hand until they thought they could remember how to keep themselves safe, children quickly became aware of what was needed, and were proud to take responsibility for their own safety. They were willing to rehearse what was important in discussion before going to the lake, and very soon they took care of the toddlers who were not yet at a stage to be able to do this.

Here we can see real education at work, where the inner motivation of the child to develop their learning is supported. Children understand the reasons why they need to behave in certain ways in order to be safe, and the result is that with this helpful guidance, which they appreciate, they find they have a great deal more freedom and a sense of pride in being allowed it. These children are being set on the journey into good community awareness and good citizenship later on. The parents are also developing effective strategies which make family life less fraught, more relaxed and enjoyable, and they are able to open up their own learning alongside their children.

These children made the transition into primary school very confidently and successfully, and were regarded as well-behaved and helpful members of the school, enthusiastic learners and hard workers. The work of this nursery school was written up in the tradition of another Froebelian, Susan Isaacs (1930, 1933), with the observations of children set out and analysed through use of current theory, and the teacher referred to as Mrs B. The first edition of the book (Athey, 1990), which brings together the key messages of this Froebelian project, remains one of the most cited publications in the early childhood literature.

The Froebel Blockplay Collaborative Research Project

A second Froebelian project is the Froebel Blockplay Collaborative Research Project. This arose from a decision by the governing body of the Froebel Educational Institute to fund a piece of work which brought up to date an aspect of the Froebelian approach to education. The director of the Centre for Early Childhood Studies, in the Froebel College (author of this chapter) was invited to put forward a proposal, and the decision was to undertake a piece of collaborative research on wooden blockplay. Initially the practitioners from the schools involved did not feel confident to share the work with the parents, but this quickly changed. This was an expensive piece of equipment for parents to buy. The parents could see how their children benefited from the social aspect of constructing with others. Children learnt to negotiate, collaborate, learn from each other, and to develop sophisticated building techniques. They began to appreciate architecture in and beyond their communities into the wider world. Parents became more relaxed about the fact that they were sending their children to school to play. They began to see that blockplay offers children possibilities to apply their knowledge of mathematics, architecture, engineering, relating to others, having and developing ideas, making stories out of their constructions, feeling proud, concentrating and being engaged and focused in their learning – and more. This Froebelian work was written up in a book edited by the dedicated and deeply committed Assistant Research Director, Pat Gura (1992).

As we saw in the previous section, and in the first chapter of this book, play is not an easy concept to understand. If this is so for practitioners who have studied it, it is even more so for parents who intuitively place it in opposition to work. The Froebelian Susan Isaacs (1930, 1933) took the view that play is in fact a child's work. This suggests, that if educators are to convince parents that play has an important contribution to make to a child's learning, then we need to get rid of the muddled thinking that surrounds it, and which causes confusion. When parents see the tangible results and impact that play has on the learning of their children, through something like wooden blockplay, supported by practitioners in observing their children at play, and seeing how through play children apply, try out, analyse, experiment and reflect on what they know, feel and relate to, they typically become enthusiastic about it.

Froebelian principles in this chapter

- Respect for parents rather than passing judgement and seeing them as deficient in their skills in bringing up their children is a key Froebelian principle.
- Parents do not have to be taught how to bring up their children. But bringing up children isolated from community is damaging to family life. Parents need to be part of a learning community in which, together with the practitioners who spend time with their children, they develop their understanding about what makes the best practice in developing children to flourish and live fulfilled lives.
- This kind of learning community empowers parents. When parents feel confident enough to enjoy the company of their children, family life offers freedom with guidance that benefits the child, the parent and the community, and eventually the wider world. Parents who are helped to develop the things which fascinate and interest their children, and who support this in their children's play, are well equipped for parenthood.
- Parents who focus on the intrinsic motivation of their babies, toddlers and young children help them to develop self-discipline, making them autonomous learners who do not rely on extrinsic rewards or higher authority to make them conform.

Reflective questions and practical actions

- Consider the differences in approach between shaping a child's behaviour and externally managing it through extrinsic reward, and supporting the natural intrinsic motivation of the child as a baby, toddler and young child to develop self-discipline
- How can you help parents, using Chapters 1 and 2, to understand the importance of play?

Introductory reading

Bruce, T., Meggitt, C. and Grenier, J. (2010) *Child Care and Education*. 5th edn. London: Hodder. Read the sections on working with parents.

Further reading

Athey, C. (1990) *Extending Thought in Young Children: A Parent–Teacher Partnership*. London: Paul Chapman Publishing.

Bruce, T. (2011a) *Early Childhood Education*. 4th edn. London: Hodder Arnold.

Gura, P. (ed.) (1992) *Exploring Learning: Young Children and Blockplay*. London: Paul Chapman Publishing.

CHAPTER 3

THE CHANGING OF THE SEASONS IN THE CHILD GARDEN

STELLA BROWN

Observations of children

Jenny was a 4-year-old child, acquiring English as a second language. She had a deep curiosity for living things in the garden and often studied mini-beasts in a magnifying 'bug box'. There was great excitement one day when she found "a creature" that was new in the garden. She immediately sought adult support to help her investigate. Other children were attracted by her enthusiasm. Together they studied the creature, talking about the size, colour and shape. They decided to take photographs to record their findings. They then used the bug box to magnify and study a little closer. Jenny was still highly motivated and insistent in her need to identify and name her creature. A member of staff suggested that they use the computer to research further. This was a successful search using technology for information. Jenny settled *and appeared to be happy that her exploration was complete. She had studied and named her find and the episode of learning and sharing with an adult and interested group seemed to be complete. Jenny however, showed autonomy in her learning. She was still interested when others had moved on. It was exciting to find her a short time later, on the floor of the verandah with paper and pens recording her observations very closely by making accurate drawings of the 'stink bug'. Even more surprising was that another, younger child, influenced by Jenny's deep motivation and passion was beside her imitating and learning from her talk and her actions. The language-rich experience of discussion and mark-making to record her findings was autonomous and fulfilling in its nature. She was able to identify another avenue to extend and develop her interest.*

In one short observation of discovery and learning, it is possible to identify the principles of curriculum design. There was depth, relevance, personalisation and choice, coherence, breadth, challenge and enjoyment and progression all in one observation. Ensuring that the child is at the centre of learning, working in a truly connected, active, flexible curriculum is key. The curricular areas or subjects covered in the example above are closely intertwined. It would not be difficult, however, to exemplify learning in science, social studies, technologies, numeracy, literacy, expressive arts, and health and well-being. A rich experience supported and developed by sensitive, knowledgeable adults, recognising a significant moment, knowing when and how to interact and when to give the child autonomy – this quiet supporting of children is Froebelian in nature.

Ensuring that the child is at the centre and leading the curriculum rather than the curriculum leading the child is crucial to our thinking. Using observation to inform development rather than an imposed curriculum leading the child is crucial. The unique element of this philosophy is its timelessness. The principles applied so long ago live on today. The application of theory and practice can be strongly reunited in meeting the requirements of curriculum design and child assessment. The relevance of observing the child and placing their needs at the centre of our active environment, of playing and working with purpose outdoors and indoors, is crucial. The encompassing importance of well-being is paramount. Fresh air, exercise, healthy eating and all aspects of the 'feel-good factor' of working co-operatively and sensing ownership and responsibility are central to good practice. The emergence of the technological era of modern-day materials and colour in everyday life are enhancements to the wealth of experiences and opportunities that now combine to create the child's world. Acknowledging change and the influences of real-life innovations is vitally important. We cannot, or should not, expect children to be unaffected by extremely strong electronic and technological innovations. We can, however, be instrumental in scaffolding the nursery environment to balance the context in order to make considered use of items such as computers, colour, cameras, or electronic toys to enhance learning and experience for life in the twenty-first century.

Froebel believed in providing real-life experiences for children at that time. He could not predict the future. Our challenge now is to provide children with the legacy of that deep-rooted knowledge of experiences that are timeless but also take account of current living and the certain knowledge that lives and work in the future will require a population that is skilled and adept with electronic innovation that is currently experiencing an extremely rapid pace of change and development.

The examples below are set out to exemplify one typical experience in each season. The garden is the crucial factor. The space and planned areas to support outdoor learning are necessary factors. The garden area, that is embedded in daily provision, that is familiar and secure, that is available to children every day, that provides continuous opportunities for learning as part of everyday nursery life is the defining element.

Reflective seasonal observations

Winter

Fiona came into nursery highly motivated after seeing a programme on television about feeding birds in winter. It was very snowy in the nursery garden. She talked about the programme she had watched and she asked 'Can we make bird cakes?' It was agreed that it was a good idea. A discussion followed, thinking about what would be needed and how to do it. Other children were beginning to take an interest in the conversation. Together a list of ingredients for bird cakes using her memory of the programme and group knowledge, with the adult scribing was made. Fiona asked if we could make them the next day. There was excitement as she talked through the plan and there was eager anticipation about the next day. The activity was set up to ensure full participation by the interested children. Step by step, sequenced pictures were created to support the learning experience. The detailed discussion continued from the previous day and there was growing anticipation about the next step of going out in the snow to choose places that might interest the birds. The process of making the cakes was very important. The application of physical skills to create a meaningful end product that was for a purpose seemed to be important to the children. They had a job to do. The growing sense of pride was tangible as the children prepared to take their contribution outdoors to help look after our bird life. There was very practical thought given to suitable locations and Fiona wanted to be able to 'look out of the window' to watch birds feeding. Once outdoors, each child was encouraged to select their own place to hang their 'cake'. The interest developed into identification of garden birds and the use of 'marks' on a chart to indicate the frequency of visiting birds.

Spring

The season plan indicated that it was time to plant potatoes. The staff planned to stimulate interest by displaying seed potatoes in a basket along with a book. There was immediate interest and lots of questions. **Jonny** *wanted to know, 'What are these?' 'What are they for?' 'What are we going to do with them?' The supporting adult was there to discuss the questions and sensitively engage the willing and interested helpers. The places suitable for planting were identified by walking around the garden and talking together about light, protection, water, play spaces and other plants. Using real tools the children dug the soil and planted the seed potatoes in the raised bed and in 'grow bags' (Figure 3.1). The children were given the task of remembering to water the potatoes (using collected rainwater) each day. The jobs gave them a sense of responsibility and ownership. The excitement of the first shoots appearing was infectious. They had empowered growth and the sense of well-being was tangible. The nurturing and caring of the plants was taken very seriously by everyone and the anticipation of growth beneath the soil as well as above was discussed widely. After a long and patient wait, the day of harvesting the crop still brought surprise. Without exception, the children showed surprise when 'they potatoes came oot that mud'.*

Figure 3.1   Time to plant the seed potatoes

Summer

Angela was very excited to discover live caterpillars in a pot in the nursery. She asked lots of questions and used a fact book with an adult to find information. She watched very closely on the first day and told other children about her discovery. At home time she took her mum to look at the caterpillars and retold factual information that she had learned that day through sensitive interaction with an adult. Her interest was consistent. Each day she observed and talked about change and size. Other children were interested but Angela began to take ownership of the caterpillars. When she arrived one day to find chrysalis in the pot instead of caterpillars she was fascinated. She had become familiar with the theory of the stages in the life cycle but the first-hand, real-life experience was profound. This sense of wonder continued through the stages. As the butterflies emerged she became totally engrossed and studied them intently. Without discussion she fetched pens and paper and began to draw. As she observed intricate detail, she made representations on paper reflecting the intensity of her interest. Generally there was eager anticipation on the day that the butterflies were to be released into the garden. Angela talked about why it was important to let them go. Her understanding was sound. However, as the butterflies flew away her mood was serious and solemn, unlike others who cheered jubilantly. Her ownership, caring and responsibility, were complete but emotionally there was also for her a sense of loss.

Autumn

Douglas was an enthusiastic helper as we prepared to harvest our crop of apples from the apple tree. He had been waiting for this day. The collecting, hunter-gatherer instinct was almost palpable as the wheelbarrows and trolleys were collected from the shed to gather the crop . There was a collective spirit as the fruit was gathered. Douglas experienced a sense of responsibility doing this job. He assumed a leadership role and helped to organise the workforce telling other children where to go and the job they should do. Interestingly, this was accepted and the adult stood back and observed the collective workers, busy at their task. One barrow was for 'rotten' fruit, that would go to the compost. Big apples were to be sorted into one and small ones into another (Figure 3.2). The adult role was minimal, using the clippers to reach the higher branches was all that was required. Listening to the workforce was informative as they talked about the size of the fruit and the quantity. They talked about the need to wash the apples because some were 'yucky' and they talked about eating some for a snack. The conversation then turned to apple pie. 'We could make apple pie.' The adult was then included as Douglas asked, 'Can we make apple pie?'

Figure 3.2   Harvest time and lots of work to do

Practical work with children and families –
the child garden

The concept of a 'children's garden' or kindergarten bears historical significance and is rich, deep and profound. The thinking and vision of early pioneers has provided a rich legacy for future generations. The philosophy of learning founded on the garden demands consideration and reflection by early years practitioners educating and supporting the growth and development of young children in the twenty-first century.

At this time of rapid change and reconsideration of curriculum development for young children in the UK, it is remarkable that the underpinning principles of the past re-emerge and in so many ways reflect the vision, wisdom, knowledge and experience of early pioneers.

Friedrich Froebel (1782–1852) created a kindergarten in Blankenburg, Germany, that reflected his philosophy of holistic learning. A place for children to learn through activity and first-hand experience using real-life tools and equipment in work and play:

> To Froebel, the garden was both literal and metaphorical. He used the word kindergarten, a garden for children, rather than the word school and saw the kindergarten

as a place where the child could develop harmony with nature. Educators would provide a rich environment for growth and would tend, nurture and cultivate each child just as a good gardener would tend a young plant. Froebel believed in a divine unity and connectedness between all living things, and it was therefore important for children to be close to nature in the outdoors environment. (Tovey, 2007: 40)

Froebel's thinking clearly linked the garden to children developing a sense of their own place in the natural world and planet Earth.

At the end of the nineteenth century Margaret McMillan was a socialist politician and a social reformer. She believed that time spent outdoors could dramatically improve children's health and that the youngest children should be the focus of attention so that her theory of potential long-lasting effects on life could be realised. She, therefore, developed her first open-air nursery school in 1914 in Deptford. Her belief was that health and education went 'hand in hand'. McMillan was a Froebelian and was influenced by Froebel's earlier observations and philosophy of holistic learning and growth in a garden environment:

McMillan spent much time making this a beautiful oasis; it was designed with the learning of children at the heart of it. And its relevance to our work today is that it was a planned space where adults played with and helped children. This children's garden was not 'thrown together'; it was not by chance that it was appropriate for young children, it was carefully planned and organised, tended and managed with the learning of children at its heart. (Bilton, 1998: 20)

The significance of teachers was thought to be crucial:

The whole value of the nursery school will depend, of course, on the teachers. They are the heart of the problem, they can give or withhold success'. (McMillan, 1919: 81, cited in Bilton, 1998: 21).

The pioneers stressed aspects of educational practice which included the importance of space, uninterrupted play, the social aspects of school, the enhancement of corporate activity and self-initiated play. (Owen, 1928, Cusden, 1938 and de Lissa, 1939, cited in Bilton, 1998: 21)

In Edinburgh, there was a strong interest in the nursery school movement and by 1930 there were nine nursery schools. The focus of interest for this 'story' lies with one of them, Tynecastle Child Garden, officially opened on 25 September 1930, by Miss Ishbel MacDonald, daughter of the Prime Minister, Ramsay MacDonald. The following is an account of her address to officially open the child garden:

I am very pleased, said Miss MacDonald, that it has been possible for me to arrange to come here on my way south to declare this Child Garden open. I am keenly interested in the nursery schools movement.

Miss MacDonald said that there were two ways of growing plants in the garden. They could grow the seeds in the beds in the garden, or sow them in boxes. The seeds grown in the garden were allowed to struggle against the difficulties that surrounded them. The seeds in the greenhouses were carefully tended and sheltered from the storms. When they were strong enough to face the storms they were planted out in rows in the garden. With those that were sown in the garden they had to allow for accidents, and some grew up such miserable specimens that they had to be weeded out and thrown away. They were not strong enough to stand against the competition of the other flowers. In the same way, many of their children had to fight against conditions which they were not strong enough to fight against. They were not weeded out and thrown away, but they had to go on living and competing with the stronger forces about them. They were unhealthy citizens. How much better it would have been if long ago they had started nursery schools, so that children could grow up with a certain amount of shelter until they were strong enough to face the storms. About 80% of the children born were healthy children. By the time they reached the age of five and went to elementary schools, about 30–40% were already diseased and delicate children, unable to benefit from the big schools provided by the authorities. They were spending millions of pounds a year in treating school children at their school clinics and in other ways. If education authorities provided more nursery schools they would have to spend less on patching up children in the elementary schools at the age of five. When there was an epidemic in the neighbourhood of a nursery school, the children from the nursery school did not get it in such a large proportion as those who were at home. This school was going to be more important than they perhaps realised. It was going to provide health and happiness for a few children in this neighbourhood, but it was also going to show what a nursery school could do and how worthwhile it was to open more of them. The nursery school was hardly out of the experimental stage yet. It should be beyond that by now. It should be established and recognised by every education authority as one step in education. The children attended regularly, had open-air surroundings, regular meals and regular rest, and learnt regular and good habits which the mothers would like but had no opportunity to teach them. One of the things the children learnt was to give and take in a little community and they would grow up the better citizens. (The *Scotsman* Digital Archive, 1930)

The Froebelian principles and influence of Margaret McMillan in England were shaping the introduction and development of care and education for young children in Edinburgh:

> Mr McKechnie, proposing a vote of thanks to Miss MacDonald, said that nursery schools were very much in the limelight. The Ministry of Health, the Board of Education, and the Scottish Education Department had all been issuing circulars, according to which the schools should be small and have a garden and a sunny aspect. (The *Scotsman* Archive, 1930)

Today, the name of the establishment is Tynecastle Nursery School but the time-honoured traditions of playing, learning and working outdoors in the garden are as significant and important as the activities that take place indoors, if not more so. This is the opinion of children, parents and staff who, together, value the wide-ranging elements of a 'green space' or oasis, in a city-centre nursery. It is fortuitous and timely that the ethos and philosophy of the Scottish *Curriculum for Excellence* (Scottish Executive, Learning and Teaching Scotland, 2009) together with the English, Welsh and Northern Irish curriculae emphasises experiences and outcomes for young children across a range of areas that combine the wealth of learning opportunities available in an environment that is beautiful, interesting, carefully designed and challenging. The reaffirmation of the trusted and time-honoured values and principles of Froebelian theory give strong historical and theoretical grounding to navigate curricular development. The theory of 'connections', that learning is not compartmentalised or separated into subjects or curricular areas, has strong reverberation today and yesterday; learning is interconnected. The knowledge and skill lies in the deep knowledge and awareness of learning and how the components connect. The role of the adult is therefore crucial.

At Tynecastle Nursery School, the school emblem is a sunflower. In order to illustrate curriculum development and the current influences on learning, including our vision for children, it was decided to create a 'curriculum map' based on the sunflower seed 'growing' in the child garden (see Figure 3.3). The child is represented by the growing seed supported by family and staff, but

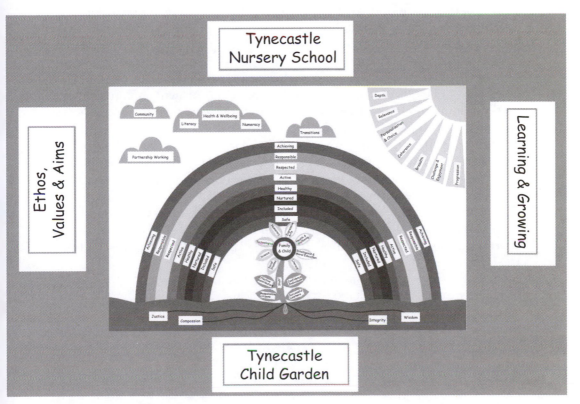

Figure 3.3 Nursery Poster

underpinned by strong roots, the values of Scottish society. The capacities and curricular areas of the Scottish *Curriculum for Excellence* are illustrated as essential parts of the flower. The sun's rays, depicting the principles of curriculum design reach out over everything. The overarching shape of the rainbow defines the eight features of Scotland's vision for children. The clouds state the necessary elements of focus and working collaboratively. All of this combined with the school's ethos, values and aims, and surrounded by the philosophy of learning and growing, helps staff and parents to consider the parts of a big picture for children today.

The seasons – a natural long-term planning model

The qualities that are provided naturally through the variety of physical conditions and changes in growth through the cycles of the year provide a strong and secure scaffolding to plan learning that will assuredly attract the attention and curiosity of children. Despite all manner of influences, interests and personal experiences, all children are affected by changing weather conditions and seasonal changes in the immediacy of the nursery garden and their world beyond. The flexible cadence of the natural world provides us with a perfect pace and rhythm for observation, investigation, exploration and reflection in a most meaningful context where children experience ownership, responsibility and autonomy for their space and place. Children begin to understand that there is an annual pattern and security in the natural world. The leaves on trees and bushes will always change from greens to a myriad of magnificent oranges, yellows, reds and browns in autumn, and without doubt they will fall to the ground but they cannot hurry the process or, indeed, prevent the course of nature. The balance of light and dark will change even though many children dislike darkness and feel less safe in a darkened atmosphere. Winter will bring colder temperatures and slow growth but the first green shoots of the snowdrops will appear, signalling further change. As spring begins, the daffodils will surprise and appeal to their sense of wonder as they discover this magnificent flower in their garden. The joy of longer, warmer days will provide a wealth of fascinating discoveries as bugs and beasts appear for safe capture and closer observation. Despite all else, this process will happen.

In a historical context this remains unchanged, the findings of the early pioneers are therefore unaffected by time, fashion or trends. The exemplification is a mere snapshot and only provides an oversimplification of a complex process. It will never be exactly the same in any year but the natural pattern of events provides us with knowledge, experience, anticipation, prediction and certain influence on learning in the child garden. This back drop provides us with the most exciting opportunity for yearly planning. Practitioners have the gift of nature to plan learning opportunities for young children in their long-term plan. To work through the certain effects and events of seasonal change, season by season, defining the labyrinth of learning opportunities and experiences within the garden provides staff, parents and children with a rich tapestry that is unaffected by all other influences and conditions of life and events. There is a colourful kaleidoscope of meaningful, tangible, flexible and rich experiences that provide significant personal understanding and knowledge of life.

The importance and significance of the quality of the garden and the way that children, parents and staff value, plan, develop and use provision cannot be underestimated. Thoughtful, enduring thinking and planning by interested, knowledgeable adults and children is crucial. Respect for the power of nature, the potential for learning in the garden and recognising children's needs, stage of learning and understanding is paramount.

Taking learning outdoors – experiences and opportunities in the child garden/outdoors today

It is extraordinary that more than a hundred years on, curriculum design is identifying the importance and power of outdoors as a crucial area for learning. In some establishments this sure and certain knowledge has lived on and been passed on through generations of early years practitioners. It is rewarding and reaffirming for those who have never doubted, but sometimes felt a need to justify their philosophy, but also exciting that, now, others may benefit from time-honoured tradition that has evolved with time to meet the needs, demands and interests of modern society. It is interesting that many of the key concepts of outdoor learning are, in fact, unaffected by trend or fashion; the profound theories of the pioneers are still relevant but may be expressed differently or be presented within curricular development materials. It is possible that experienced practitioners enjoy the reward and confidence of building on and improving practice. The timeless elements include aspects such as the importance of spending time outdoors, experiencing nature and the seasons in changeable weather conditions, children taking responsibility and learning through first-hand experiences, children using real tools and equipment to complete work tasks, adults observing children to inform future learning and experiences, and careful consideration and design of areas to fulfil opportunities for a range of experiences including adventurous play.

The framework curriculum documents of each country of the UK, and indeed in countries throughout the world where there are national documents guiding practice in the early years, although they each have the individual hallmarks and flavour of their cultural and historic traditions, also share much in common. The Scottish *Curriculum for Excellence* exemplifies child-centred, active learning for all children and young people, not only in the early years but throughout life:

> This is undoubtedly an exciting time in Scottish education. There is a real drive for all children and young people to achieve across a broad educational experience. As we look to their future, and the challenges children and young people face, they need the values to choose to live more sustainable lives and these can be successfully developed by learning outdoors. (Scottish Executive, Learning and Teaching Scotland, 2007: 1)

This is powerful indeed for all educationists but for the early years practitioners, laying the foundations for immediate learning and future developments is of high significance:

> Outdoor learning is not, and should not be, an end in itself, but should be embedded in *A Curriculum for Excellence 3–18*. It must offer core experiences to children and young people, regularly and routinely, every day and then through their transitions from pre-school education to adulthood. (Scottish Executive, Learning and Teaching Scotland, 2007: 1)

In a well-planned garden context or outdoor area, the range of learning opportunities in the flexible, dynamic, unpredictable 'world' of the garden is beyond parameters. Outdoors, children can experience the whole curriculum in an active, child-centred context that embeds core experiences on a daily basis providing regular and routine access to rich play and learning across the curriculum. The fact that children can choose outdoor play every day and develop autonomy in their environment is of central importance.

A carefully designed, planned and well maintained outdoor space, based on observation of children is the key to the potentially rich landscape for play, discovery, exploration, enjoyment, challenge, experience and learning. It can be a place that creates opportunities for children to experience physical activity, a place to observe and connect with nature, a place to look after, a place to be responsible for, a place for ownership, a place for fresh air and exercise, a place to work, a place to co-operate and collaborate, a place to make friendships, a place to be alone or with friends, a place to develop confidence, a place to take risks, a place to express feelings, a place to imagine, a place to make noise, a place just to be – a seemingly endless list of 'places' where the needs of children are central to the environment or context for learning. In the rich, creative context of the garden it is then possible to apply the principles of curriculum design as described in the Scottish *Curriculum for Excellence* 3–18 (Scottish Executive, Learning and Teaching Scotland, 2009):

- Challenge and enjoyment
- Breadth
- Progression
- Depth
- Personalisation and choice
- Coherence
- Relevance.

Children will benefit from consideration of these principles when practitioners give due consideration to the value of outdoor experiences and apply the principles as values in today's context. The 'interconnectedness' of curricular areas can be exemplified through observation of children at play in the child garden.

'Things go round in circles.' We go back to the beginning of this school's history when it was recognised in the opening speech that an analogy can be made of a seed growing and flourishing to a child learning and growing, if the conditions are right. It is a privilege to create those ideal conditions for children in our care to ensure that each one has the best possible opportunity for rich growth to reach their full learning potential.

Froebelian principles in this chapter

- Recognition of the uniqueness of each child's capacity and potential. It is crucial that children have choice in order to develop their uniqueness. The qualities of the indoor and outdoor learning environments in the nursery setting fully support each child to achieve their own personal learning potential. There is value in observing a child indoors, taking note of behaviour, body language, language and motivation, and then again outdoors. For some children the garden might be the significant element that unlocks full potential. The value of a complete learning environment, a fully integrated indoor/outdoor space, that is available to children simultaneously creates the conditions for each child's capacity and potential to be recognised and fulfilled.
- An holistic view of each child's development. The view of a whole child, considering all aspects of development and learning in the widest sense can be truly considered in the context of the indoor/outdoor environment as detailed throughout this chapter.
- Recognition of the importance of play as a central integrating element in a child's development and learning. Play is a central defining feature of a child's development and learning. The wide and varied opportunities for play in the garden and outdoors are as important if not more so, than indoor experiences. Freedom for children to explore through play demands consideration as adults plan, create and support any context for learning.
- An ecological view of humankind in the natural world. This principle is at the core of all other features of development and learning in young children and remains unchanged for generations. It is, without question an integral part of the deep and rich learning that, if nurtured in our youngest children, grows into an important manifestation of care and consideration of significant and important issues for the future.
- Recognition of childhood in its own right. The 'here and now' of childhood learning is critical in our thinking. It is not a preparation for the future or a precursor to any other stage in life. The values, attention, attitudes and

investment in our young children and the qualities that are promoted through early learning experiences cannot be underestimated.

- Recognition of the child as part of a family and a community. A child cannot operate and develop alone. The interaction of family and the community that is significant has to be recognised and respected. Working together as a supporting and positive framework scaffolds the human network for children. Relationships that respect one another and provide security and collaboration ensure best conditions for growth. The nursery community, working together with a child and parents/carers both indoors and outdoors creates a rich, shared experience that can then be extended to the wider local community and beyond.

Reflective questions and practical actions

- The garden area that is embedded in daily provision, that is familiar and secure, that is available to children every day, that provides continuous opportunities for learning as part of everyday nursery life is a defining element of provision. Consider the role of the adult as a crucial participant in children's learning in this context.
- Consider the outdoor area in your own learning environment in relation to the four seasons. Are there further opportunities to maximise learning through the natural cadence of seasonal events and conditions throughout a whole year? Try creating an audit of the four seasons and the opportunities for learning that can be developed within a natural context.

Further reading

Bilton, H. (1998) *Outdoor Play in the Early Years: Management and Innovation*. London: David Fulton.

Bruce, T. (2004) *Developing Learning in Early Childhood*. London: Paul Chapman Publishing.

Community Playthings, (2008) *I Made a Unicorn! Open-ended Play with Blocks and Simple Materials*. Robertsbridge, E. Sussex: Community Playthings.

Ouvry, M. (2000) *Exercising Muscles and Minds: Outdoor Play and the Early Years Curriculum*. London: The National Early Years Network.

Scottish Executive, Learning and Teaching Scotland (2007) *Taking Learning Outdoors, Partnerships for Excellence*. Glasgow: Learning and Teaching Scotland.

Scottish Excutive, Learning and Teaching Scotland (2009) *Curriculum for Excellence 3–18*. Glasgow. Learning and Teaching Scotland.

Tovey, H. (2007) *Playing Outdoors: Spaces and Places, Risk and Challenge*. London: Open University Press.

CHAPTER 4

ADVENTUROUS AND CHALLENGING PLAY OUTDOORS

HELEN TOVEY

Watch children playing outdoors and they seem to seek out and enjoy scary, risky situations, such as climbing high, sliding fast, balancing precariously or hanging upside down. They enjoy pushing their own limits and testing out what they can do or what they can nearly do.

Observing children's risk-taking and adventurous play

Example 1

A 2-year-old sets off into the garden with a bundle of clothes pegs. Finding some tall plant stems he set about trying to fix the clothes pegs to each stem.

Figure 4.1   Adventurous play includes pushing boundaries. How far can I go? How safe is this?

On finding a thistle he recoiled his hand in surprise at the sharp prickles but immediately touched it again, fascinated and joyous at the new experience.

Example 2

A mixed-age group of children in a workplace nursery enjoyed playing on a rope swing. They soon discovered if they twisted the rope round and then let go, the swing, with a child inside, rotated at great speed.

Example 3

Children on a visit to Wimbledon Common enjoyed the challenge of climbing fallen trees. This involved finding handholds and footholds to navigate their way up the steep angle of the tree. A 4-year-old girl climbed near to the top then hesitated on finding some loose material. She decided against climbing

Figure 4.2   Challenging play involves some risk and willingness to 'have a go'

further and embarked on the more challenging descent testing the footholds as she went (see Figure 4.1).

Example 4

A group of boys fixed a rope and pulley onto the branch of a tree so that they could lift a bucket of twigs and leaves into the tree. They used trial and error to manoeuvre the rope risking the possibility of the bucket crashing down, and laughing when it did (see Figure 4.2).

All these examples illustrate how young children, at any age, seek out and enjoy challenging experiences where risk, uncertainty and adventure are central to the play. As ready opportunities for such adventurous play have declined in recent years, an early years setting may be one of the few places where children can test and push their limits in a challenging outdoor environment.

Some characteristics of adventurous, challenging play

- Play involving height, motion and speed.
- Inverting usual body posture, for example, tipping, spinning, rolling and hanging upside down.
- Joyfulness in precariousness and unpredictability such as balancing along a rickety bridge.
- Deliberately seeking out scary situations whether imagined or real, such as hiding in a dark place or playing 'monsters'.
- Being daring, innovative, testing and pushing limits.
- Experiencing new and, therefore, unpredictable situations which include some risk and excitement, for example, feeding a fire with sticks, treading through thick mud, lifting heavy buckets on a pulley wheel.

There can be great joy when risk itself is the central feature of the play and the main reason to continue. The simultaneous experience of risk and challenge, fear and exhilaration, feelings of being on the borders of being out of control, characterises such play. We can see this in babies' precarious delight in being thrown up in the air, bounced vigorously or tipped backwards, in young children's joy in balancing along a wobbly bridge or in older children swinging on the end of a rope. Many adults' enjoyment of activities such as skiing, zip-wire riding or sledging can evoke similar exhilarating enjoyment.

Such play has some links to what Roger Caillois calls 'ilynx' or 'dizzy play' (Kalliala, 2006). Ilynx is the Greek word for whirling water, and dizzy play often has this freewheeling, spinning, exhilarating enjoyment. Caillois identifies what he refers to as 'voluptuous panic' that is the simultaneous feelings of joy and fear which such play can engender. He argues that such experiences are often important elements of group camaraderie, friendship and social cohesion.

Adventurousness and daring can also be seen in imagined play worlds where children deliberately enjoy scaring themselves through monster play, or escaping the big bad wolf. Play outdoors often involves adventures, chases, escapes, captures and rescues. Danger, or the fear of danger, can underpin much of the play and earthquakes, floods, fires, poison, car crashes are frequent themes of such play. Feelings of bravado, daring and power can also underpin much superhero play. In such play children venture into new, unexplored territory where they can safely explore themes of good and evil, fear and joy, life and death, power and powerlessness.

Adventurous play outdoors

Outdoors offers rich opportunities for adventurous and challenging play. The open space and variety of terrain, offer unique challenges, with rocks or fallen tree trunks to clamber over, low branches to crawl under, long grass or tangled bushes to creep through and plenty of nooks and crannies to investigate. Children can push their bodies to their limits whether climbing, balancing or swinging, in a way which is much more difficult indoors. The dynamic, unpredictable nature of the outdoor area with its ever-changing patterns of weather and seasons offers wonder and surprise, inviting curiosity and investigation. The open-endedness of the outdoor environment offers problems to be solved as well as materials to be combined creatively. A well-planned outdoor area has pathways, hiding areas, tunnels, concealed entrances and exits which invite exploration and a sense of adventure. A rich outdoor area offers infinite possibilities for challenge and adventure, and the chance to discover or create what Froebel referred to as 'new worlds' (Froebel, in Lilley, 1967: 126).

All too often attention focuses on the potential risk or danger of children's play outdoors without balancing it against the potential benefits. However Froebel recognised the value of children's adventurous play outdoors. He emphasised the importance of first-hand experience and the integrated way in which children learn. These principles can be seen in this extract from his writings which describe an imagined conversation about the possible danger of a child climbing a tree.

> To climb a new tree is … to discover a new world. If we could remember our joy when in childhood we looked out beyond the cramping limits of our immediate surroundings we should not be so insensitive as to call out 'come down, you will fall'. One learns to protect oneself from falling by looking over and around a place as well as by physical movement and the ordinary thing certainly looks quite different from above. Ought we not then to give the boy opportunities for an enlargement of his view which will broaden his thoughts and feelings?
>
> 'But he will be reckless and I shall never be free of anxiety about him.'
>
> No, the boy whose training has always been connected with the gradual development of his capacities will attempt only a little more than he has already been able to do and will come safely through all these dangers. It is the boy who does not know his strength and the demands made on it who is likely to venture beyond his experience and run into unsuspected danger. (Froebel, in Lilley, 1967: 126)

Within this short extract Froebel makes some very significant points about the value of adventurous play outdoors. He focuses not on the risk, but on the benefit of such activity. He recognises the sense of joy and freedom associated with pushing the boundaries beyond the limits of everyday experience and of venturing into a new world where things look different. Such experience is educative as it opens up new perspectives for example of height and distance. Everyday life is transformed when seen from a different perspective and this helps to broaden children's thinking, understanding and feelings about the world. Such learning is achieved though self-activity where children can find out how their bodies work in a challenging context by testing their nerve, strength and skill. They are motivated to push out their own boundaries by the thrill of the activity and often the exuberant camaraderie of others. Physical, cognitive, personal and emotional learning are integrated in one activity.

Froebel also makes a very fundamental point that children who experience increasing challenge in play are safer than children who have been protected from risks. It is children who lack experience and are unaware of the possibilities and limitations of their own bodies who will be more likely to come to harm.

This reflects a view of children as active, competent learners, not passive, helpless learners. It shows an attitude of trusting children to be able to do things for themselves rather than underestimating children's capabilities. Overall it shows a view of children as adventure-seekers, looking for new challenges and problems to overcome, and of adults who need to be sensitive to this sense of adventure rather than undermining it with negative comments such as 'come down, you'll fall'.

Froebel's views on the value of what he termed 'brave and daring' play can also be seen in later pioneers who were influenced by Froebel. For example Margaret McMillan argued that children should be able to play 'bravely and adventurously' in 'a provocative environment where new chances are made possible' (McMillan, 1930: 78). She created a richly challenging outdoor environment in her nursery school in a disadvantaged area of London. The garden included wild areas, digging areas, junk heaps and trees, which she described as the best climbing equipment of all. She also included steps as she noted how much they were used and enjoyed by toddlers as they practised going up and down.

Susan Isaacs, who drew on Froebel's ideas as well as contemporary psychoanalytic theories, developed a school for advantaged children in Cambridge in the 1920s. The children had open access to a garden which was a source of curiosity, investigation, creativity and imagination. It offered challenge and potential risk as children could climb trees, use real tools, dig in deep sandpits, operate taps, make small fires and play adventurously. Like Froebel before her, she argued that freedom and responsibility, risk and safety are inseparable. Providing free access to challenging contexts empowered the children to develop the skills to be safe and she described how children 'climbed trees and ladders, used tools and handled fire and matches far more freely than is commonly allowed, and with complete impunity – partly no doubt, because of our careful supervision but largely also because their skill and poise became so good under these conditions' (Isaacs, 1930: 25).

Similarly, Marjorie Allen, better known as Lady Allen of Hurtwood, a landscape architect, was also influenced by Froebelian approaches to children's play and learning both in the UK and in Denmark. She brought the concept of the 'adventure playground' to the UK having visited an exciting Froebelian playground in Copenhagen. She defined the adventure playground as a creative play area with a wealth of waste material and no fixed equipment. It was a place where children could dig, build houses, experiment with sand, water or fire and play games of adventure and make believe. She argued that:

> Small children need a place where they can develop self reliance, where they can test their limbs, their senses and their brain, so that brain, limbs and senses gradually become obedient to their will. If during these early years a child is deprived of the opportunity to educate himself by trial and error, by taking risks and by making friends, he may … lose confidence in himself and lose his desire to become self reliant. Instead of learning security he becomes fearful and withdrawn. (Allen, 1968: 14)

Like Froebel she argued that when children are deprived of opportunities for adventurous play and risk-taking they can become dependent on the judgement of others and by implication less safe because of their limited experience of challenging situations.

All of these pioneers built on and developed Froebel's ideas. In their different ways they argued that adventurous play and risk-taking are essential elements of children's play and learning outdoors and that without opportunities for such play children are more at risk of danger.

What are the benefits of risk taking and adventurous play?

Contemporary research offers justification for the importance of risk-taking and adventurous play. Risk-taking is part of life. We assess and manage risks as part of everyday living and learn to weigh up possible risks against the benefits. We learn ways of doing things safely to minimise possible harm. Babies would never learn to crawl, negotiate steps, stand up, run, ride a bike, and so on without being prepared to take a risk, to tumble and to learn from the consequences. Learning to navigate space, people and objects requires risk and a willingness to make and learn from mistakes.

This willingness to take risks is an important learning disposition. Research by Carole Dweck (2000), for example, emphasises the importance of what she terms a 'mastery' approach to learning – a disposition to have a go, try something out and relish challenge, in contrast to a 'helpless' approach characterised by fearfulness and fear of failure. There is a danger that when we repeatedly say to children 'mind out', 'be careful', 'don't do that' or 'come down, you'll fall' we can inadvertently develop this 'helpless' attitude to learning by communicating our own anxiety. To have a good disposition to learn requires confidence, competence and a willingness to have a go. Play outdoors motivates children to extend their own boundaries, to be adventurous, to explore a little further and to engage with risk in a supportive environment. Outdoor environments where children are discouraged from taking risks, where adults themselves are anxious and fearful, are less likely to develop the disposition to persist, to see challenges as problems to enjoy rather than things to fear.

Risk-taking is part of the tool kit of effective learners (Claxton, 1999). Learning is not a linear pathway with one route and one destination. Rather, it is a meandering route of trial and error, a multitude of possible pathways. Venturing in the mind, exploring ideas, considering possible alternatives, daring to be creative, hypothesising possible explanations, hazarding a guess and risking failure are all important features of learning, and the more opportunities children have for this physical and mental meandering the richer their thinking. At the same time when children engage in activities which are particularly daring, scary or challenging their concentration is highly focused and intense. When safety depends on the success of your actions then all other detail is screened out and a heightened awareness of every move is achieved. When the challenge is low there is less need for such intense focus.

As in other aspects of play, risk-taking allows children to vary the familiar, to try out new ways of doing things and to be innovative for example by finding new ways of coming down the slide, or rolling a tyre. Bruner has argued that such play contributes to greater flexibility of thinking as new combinations of behaviour can be tried. Such flexibility can be important in innovative and creative thinking (Claxton, 1999). Adventurous play outdoors can offer rich opportunities for children to combine materials and ideas, and pursue seemingly irrational ideas such as rolling down a slope inside a barrel or transforming an unsteady plank into a galloping horse.

Play outdoors often involves vigorous movements such as swinging, tipping, hanging and rolling, where normal balance and posture is distorted. Research by Penny Greenland (2006) suggests that such movement play is vital in stimulating young children's vestibular and proprioceptive senses, that is their sense of balance and awareness of their own body in space. She argues that the absence of such physically challenging play can contribute to clumsiness, attention problems and later learning difficulties. The connection between movement and cognition was central to Froebel's philosophy. Whole body experiences of a varied terrain outdoors are highly important for the development of key mathematical and scientific concepts (Athey, 1990). For example sliding head first down a slide offers experience of such things as direction, gradient, speed and concepts of head first or even head first backwards. Swinging on a rope can provide experiences of energy, forces, gravity, speed, distance, cause and effect. Confining children to flat rubberised safety surfaces denies children essential experience required for such rich conceptual learning.

Research on children's play in nature kindergartens in Norway (Fjortoft, 2004) indicates that children who experience wild, rough ground with lots of uneven surfaces, boulders for scrambling over, trees to climb and bushes to hide in are more developed physically than children who play in conventional 'flat' playgrounds. This is because the environment affords opportunities for a much wider variety of physical movement than can be found in a more conventional playground. The more varied the terrain, the greater the variety of play opportunities and therefore movements. Play was also found to be more collaborative, sustained with fewer disputes than in conventional play areas. Children's health was improved and they had fewer absences. This suggests that it is not just play outside which has beneficial effects but that particular qualities of the play environment have significant benefits on children's play, health and learning.

Biologists, Spinka et al. (2001) suggest that adventurous play is characteristic of play in all mammals and serves as 'training for the unexpected'. They argue that players deliberately put themselves in disadvantageous positions and that novelty and risk add to the intensity and pleasure of the play. Players switch easily between well-controlled movements and those where they experience being on the edge of out-of-control. Such play, they argue, increases the range and versatility of movements and helps players cope physically and emotionally with unexpected events.

Controlled exposure to some risks also appears to have a protective effect. For example Kloep and Hendry (2007) draw on Rutter's notion of 'steeling' experiences, and argue that mistakes, providing the consequences are not too severe, can offer protection against the negative effect of future failure. Managing fear and uncertainty and holding your nerve when feeling on the edge of out of control are important aspects of emotional well-being and resilience.

Froebel made much the same point, arguing that children should be brought up to bear minor afflictions so as to be able to endure more serious hardships. This is not an argument for exposure to over-challenging environments in the interest of 'character building' or 'toughening up' as too much challenge can be daunting and even frightening to many children. Instead, the environment, including the adults within it should support individual children in the challenges which they set themselves and should be flexible enough to offer sufficient challenge for the risk-cautious as well as the risk-seekers. Risk should be seen from a child's perspective, for example, stretching out a hand to touch a wriggling worm for the first time might seem very risky and daring for a 2-year-old.

This section has looked at the benefits of risk-taking and adventurous play. However, it would be wrong to think that risk-taking is all positive. Often because of lack of experience children, and indeed adults, can learn to take risks which are inappropriate, which border on recklessness or which put themselves or others at risk of injury. As in many areas of learning, children need the guidance of experienced others who can help them recognise and manage serious risk, teach safe ways of doing things, but who also encourage a positive disposition to adventure and challenge.

Creating an environment for challenging, adventurous play

The essence of an environment for challenging, adventurous play is that it is flexible, open-ended, provocative, and rich in potential for exploration, discovery, imagination and wonder. It should allow opportunity for children to experience uncertainty and unpredictability, to venture further than they have gone before, and create their own voyages of discovery. It should be fluid and dynamic rather than static and unyielding, with adults who celebrate children's competence and share with children an adventurous spirit. There is no single approach to a challenging play environment, nevertheless it is likely to include the following:

- Experience of the natural world – bushes to hide in, trees to climb, trails and pathways to follow, places to explore and to hide in. Natural materials such as boulders, stones, wood chips, soil, sand and water to explore and create with.
- A varied terrain with boulders, logs, slopes, ditches, ladders, tunnels and slides to provide a wide range of movement experiences.
- Opportunities for children to swing, slide, hang upside down, balance, crawl, clamber, tumble, romp and roll. Resources should be flexible enough to ensure challenge for the most timid and the most adventurous.
- Loose parts and open-ended recycled materials such as crates, boxes, blankets, wheels, planks, lengths of guttering, tubes, and so on. Such props can offer increasingly challenging opportunities for creative and collaborative construction, as they can be combined in many different ways. They also offer new problems to solve.
- Opportunity to move at increasingly fast speeds whether on rope swings, riding down slopes on wheeled toys or sliding down steep slides.
- Resources which offer the experience of instability such as rockers, swing bridges, rope bridges. These offer unpredictability and sense of risk with little likelihood of danger.

Roles of the educators

Despite the importance of a challenging environment, ultimately what makes a real difference to children's opportunities for adventurous play is not so much the provision but the attitudes and approaches of the educators. Research in New Zealand, for example, found that adults who enjoyed being outside, who were interested in physical play and who took a sensitive and liberal approach to supervision, helped children to find challenges that felt satisfyingly 'scary' but which did not put them in a position of hazard (Stephenson, 2003).

My own research in the UK (Tovey, 2010) suggested that when practitioners felt supported within their teams and recognised the positive features of adventurous play and risk-taking, they were more confident in offering challenging experiences. When practitioners felt unsupported by senior staff, anxious about blame and possible litigation and less aware of the benefits, they were more likely to curtail adventurous play. Paradoxically, these risk-control measures seemed to increase practitioners' anxiety outdoors, maybe because of the intensity of focus on potential danger. Restricting risk-taking also appeared to increase children's attempts to take risks resulting in conflict with the practitioners, who viewed their search for challenge as challenging behaviour.

Working with parents and families

Froebel argued that home, kindergarten and community should be closely connected and in harmony. It is hard for children to bridge a gap between very different attitudes and expectations, for example, if they are encouraged to be adventurous by some adults but reprimanded by others. Although there will always be some differences in attitudes towards adventurous play, with gender and culture sometimes shaping those differences, nevertheless a shared approach can only be achieved through respectful dialogue which opens up the issues of risk and safety for discussion and debate. Parents are often blamed for being excessively cautious, or indeed litigious, but evidence does not necessarily support this view (Gill, 2007). Rather, parents will have many different perspectives, concerns and experiences but will share with practitioners a desire that their children should learn to be safe and should also develop confidence. Many settings are now opening up a debate with parents, governors and the wider community about the value of challenging play and the dangers of overemphasising safety. Listening to parents' anxieties and finding out about individual children's experiences of playing outside is one way to start such a debate. One setting, for example, used a slide show of photographs in the entrance hall to engage parents in discussion about risk and safety alongside this quote from the UK Health and Safety Executive: 'We must not lose sight of the important developmental role of play in pursuit of the unachievable goal of absolute safety' (cited in Ball et al. 2008: 117).

It is therefore important that practitioners engage parents and the wider community in discussing issues around risk and safety in play outdoors. This is essential if shared understandings are to be achieved and parents seen as partners rather than potential critics.

In conclusion a Froebelian approach to adventurous challenging play outdoors involves the following key principles:

- *Having realistically high expectations of what children are able to do.* This means knowing children well enough to make informed decisions as to when it might be necessary to intervene and when it is better to be quietly watchful.
- *Seeing children as adventure-seekers and risk-takers.* This means tuning into children's intentions and supporting them in finding safe ways of achieving what they want to do. For example helping children collaborate in using a stepladder safely in order to reach the top of a tall construction.

- *Fostering a 'can do' culture with a positive approach to challenge*, seeing it as something to be relished, rather than feared. This will involve modelling a flexible innovative approach to situations 'that's a good idea, let's try it' rather than 'No, we're not allowed.'
- *Making sure that there is enough time and space for children to be adventurous outdoors*. Too many children and too little time outdoors can create hazardous conditions as children seek adventure but lack the opportunity and experience to develop and sustain safe ways of playing.
- *Teaching children safe ways of doing things*. For example, ways of controlling speed on a steep slide, safe ways of using a saw at the woodwork table, always using a friend to help carry a ladder or a long stick. My great nephew at 1-year-old had been taught to crawl backwards down the steep stairs in his house. For a few months he used this technique whenever he came across even a small step indoors or outdoors.
- *Helping children assess risk for themselves*. For example, children can learn to test out the stability and strength of a tree branch before putting all their weight on it.
- *Talking about risk and safety in everyday meaningful contexts*. For example, 'coming down backwards might be a safer way to do that' or 'how can we make the ladder more steady?' This also means being prepared to say a firm 'no that's dangerous because …' in the rare situations it is needed. Children can feel safer to take risks and be adventurous when there are reasonable boundaries.

Finally, if we deny children the opportunities for adventurous play we may inadvertently risk creating a generation of children who may be either reckless in their pursuit of adventure and excitement or risk averse, lacking the confidence and skills to be safe but also lacking the disposition to be adventurous, creative and innovative in their thinking. As Froebel said, children who experience risk and adventure at their own pace discover 'new worlds' and, in the end, are safer than those who are denied such experiences.

Froebelian Principles in this chapter

- Rich, first hand, meaningful experience is central to adventurous learning.
- Open ended materials offer rich scope for play, creativity and imagination.
- Learning is an integrated and connected whole.
- Children's abilities to do things for themselves should be respected and encouraged
- Education should develop children's autonomy and self confidence
- An environment should be physically and intellectually challenging promoting exploration, enquiry, discovery, imagination and wonder.
- Children learn through their own activity as well as through the actions and guidance of others.

Reflective questions

- Did you experience adventurous play outdoors? To what extent are these experiences available for children today?
- To what extent can we empower children to assess risk for themselves?
- How much does gender influence attitudes to adventurous play? Is risk-taking encouraged more in boys' than in girls' play?
- Are you able to make provision for experiences which children find satisfyingly 'scary'?
- How can you make provision for children with disabilities to experience adventurous play, for example, the exhilaration of moving at speed?

Introductory reading

Ball, D., Gill, T. and Spiegal, B. (2008) *Managing Risk in Play Provision: Implementation Guide*. Nottingham: Department for Children, Schools and Families and Department for Culture, Media and Sport.

Knight, S. (2011) *Risk and Adventure in Early Years Outdoor Play. Learning from Forest Schools*. London: Sage.

Lindon, J. (2011) *Too Safe for their Own Good? Helping Children Learn about Risk and Skills*. 2nd edn. London: National Children's Bureau.

Further reading

Allen, M. (Lady Allen of Hurtwood) (1968) *Planning for Play*. London: Thames and Hudson.

Athey, C. (1990) *Extending Thought in Young Children: A Parent–Teacher Partnership*. London: Paul Chapman Publishing.

Bundy, A., Luckett, T., Tranter, P., ; Naughton, A., Wyver, S., Razen, J. and Spies, G. (2009) The risk is that there is no risk: a simple, innovative intervention to increase children's activity levels, *International Journal of Early Years Education*, 17(1): 33–45.

Caillois, R. (2001) *Man, Play and Games*. Trans. M. Barash. Urbana, IL: University of Illinois Press.

Claxton, G. (1999) *Wise Up: The Challenge of Life-Long Learning*. London: Bloomsbury.

Dweck, C. (2000) *Self Theories: Their Role in Motivation, Personality and Development*. Hove: Psychology Press.

Fjortoft, I. (2004) 'Landscape as playscape. The effects of natural environments on children's play and motor development', *Children Youth and Environments*, 14(2).

Gill, T. (2007) *No Fear: Growing Up in a Risk Averse Society.* London: Calouste Gulbenkian Foundation.

Greenland, P. (2006) 'Physical development', in T. Bruce (ed.) *Early Childhood: A Guide for Students.* London: Sage Publications.

Kalliala, M. (2006) *Play Culture in a Changing World.* Maidenhead: Open University Press.

Kloep, M. and Hendry, L. (2007) '"Over-protection, over-protection, over-protection!" Young people in modern Britain', *Psychology of Education Review*, 31(2): 4–8.

Little, H. (2006) 'Children's risk-taking behaviour: implications for early childhood policy and practice', *International Journal of Early Years Education*, 14(2): 141–54.

Sandseter, E. (2007) 'Categorising risky play: how can we identify risk-taking in children's play?', *European Early Childhood Research*, 15(2): 237–52.

Sandester, E. (2009) 'Children's expressions of exhilaration and fear in risky play', *Contemporary Issues in Early Childhood*, 10(2) 92–106.

Spinka, M., Newberry, R. and Bekoff, M. (2001) 'Mammalian play: training for the unexpected', *The Quarterly Review of Biology*, 76(2): 141–68.

Stephenson, A. (2003) 'Physical risk taking: dangerous or endangered?', *Early Years* 23(1): 35–43.

Tovey, H. (2007) *Playing Outdoors: Spaces and Places, Risk and Challenge.* Maidenhead: Open University Press

Tovey, H. (2010) 'Playing on the edge: perceptions of risk and danger in outdoor play', in P. Broadhead, J. Howard and E. Woods (eds), *Play and Learning in the Early Years: from Research to Practice.* London: Sage Publications.

CHAPTER 5

OFFERING CHILDREN FIRST-HAND EXPERIENCES THROUGH FOREST SCHOOL: RELATING TO AND LEARNING ABOUT NATURE

LYNN MCNAIR

Friedrich Froebel emphasised the educational importance of outdoor learning and the forest school experience as a natural extension to Froebel's philosophy in the modern-day context.

Observations of children

In the interests of the children I have still another request to make – that you would record in writing the most important facts about each separate child. (An extract from Froebel's letter, in Poesche, 1981: Letter VII)

Observing 'each separate child' in nature is a privilege. A child is by impulse a naturalist and being in the natural environment develops and nurtures a side of

Figure 5.1   Satisfying the yearning for upward desires, Paloma, Mia and Natalie confidently climb the trees at forest school

the child that we may never come to know, for example, when in nature the child experiences freedom, freedom to explore, freedom from the adult world, a separate peace (this is discussed in more detail later) (Figure 5.1). Peace found in nature extends the child's spiritual inner life.

Forest school leaders (and other adults) have observed and recorded the child's delight in watching ants and worms and reported how children appreciate the miracles of nature; and forest school leaders have noted the child may communicate more freely after the forest school experience, and they report, on site, the child might explore a space alone, content to be with nature.

As Froebel commented, through the observation of children he discovered so very much about the young learner; in the following extract Froebel expresses his deep understanding of the child's drive to discover more and more:

> He helps look after animals and makes things for the house, he shares in the chopping, sawing, piling of the wood. Question after question crowds out of his enquiring mind – how? why? when? what for? – and any passably satisfactory answer opens up a new world for him. (Lilley, 1967: 125)

A child may pick up clay from the ground, peacefully rolling and forming the clay, until the child creates a creature, such as a snail, providing the adult with insight into the child's complex and divergent learning style(s) and understanding.

Another child may never have an end product, but may spend hours rolling the clay, enfolded in this is deep contemplation, about what, we may never know. It is a joy to observe children in this way. Uninterrupted time of observing; there is no need for words, just peaceful respectful, reciprocal solitude. However, Froebel noted the adult may need to at times intervene: 'The contribution of the sensitive, interested and skilled adult is indirect on the whole, but at times adults also need to take a direct role, otherwise the children's play is less rich' (Gura, 1992: 20).

Froebel believed in the child, if the child chose to offer an explanation of what he or she is doing, or perhaps decide to ask the adult a question, Froebel saw it as the role of the adult educator to sensitively respond. At forest school there is time for these discussions. As Froebel informs us 'this opens up a new world for him' (Lilley, 1967: 125).

Practical work with the children and families

Are forest schools a Froebelian idea?

The main aim of the forest school movement, which began in Sweden during the 1950s was to teach children about the natural world. The upsurge of interest was later adopted in Denmark, then subsequently in the UK in 1995.

We need only reflect on Froebel's ideas of learning through the beauty of nature, the glory of life, combined with his 'freedom and guidance' interaction to see clearly the roots and origins of forest school. Another link may be the naming of the forest school in Denmark, originally named 'bornehaven' and developed into skogsbornehaven, wood kindergarten and naturbornehaven – nature kindergarten. And that while Froebel acknowledged the child's natural curiosity provoked learning and that the child is, indeed, skilled and capable of self-activity (as mentioned above) the role of the adult is critical to the education process.

The following extract from Lilley illustrates Froebel's intention about the 'teaching of' nature to children:

> To the objection that schoolchildren in the country are out of doors all day long I reply that this does not mean that they live in and with Nature. Many adults as well as children treat Nature as one ordinarily treats the air: one lives in it while knowing almost nothing about it. Children who spend all their time in the open air may still observe nothing of the beauties of Nature and their influence on the human heart. (Lilliey, 1967: 146)

Hence from this one can easily see the influence of Froebel on the forest school movement.

Forest schools can take many forms, for example, it does not have to be held in a woodland area. Our forest school is held in a 'wild site' that belongs to the City of Edinburgh Council and is under the auspices of the Scottish Wildlife Trust (SWT). It is a short 5-minute walk from our centre (it may be important, and worthy of mention here that most early years environments will have a little treasure of land somewhere close, somewhere tucked discretely away that would make an ideal location for the forest school experience).

Our site has historical significance as one of the 'green lungs' which Patrick Geddes (1854–1932) established in the nineteenth century. Geddes was a botanist, sociologist, educator, artist and extraordinary town planner of the Old Town of Edinburgh, also known as one of the founders of environmental education. Consequently, Geddes's theory of education cannot be separated from the garden. For example, according to Welter, 'Forms of life and their emergence and development in interaction with the environment were [a] major interest of Geddes' (2002: 2).

Geddes's ideas of holism were well known, based on hand (physical/manual), heart (compassion/political) and head (learning/psychology/analytical) and throughout his life's work, he connected diverse subjects and fields of knowledge. In addition, and of significance, Geddes played a role in establishing the network of kindergartens that would become known as Edinburgh's Nursery Schools.

During the Second World War our site was covered in concrete and later became an adventure playground. The SWT took over the site in 1982, by which time it was derelict. Now, most of the concrete has been broken up, two large composts have been created, paths cleared and chippings lain, trees and hedges planted, a pond and a wildflower meadow established and, more recently, a bumblebee border introduced.

We now take great care of this site to ensure that the disruption of fauna and flora is kept to a minimum, for example, tadpoles are carefully lifted from the pond and shown to the children and then are returned gently.

Our story is reminiscent of Lileen Hardy's reflections. In a *Diary of a Free Kindergarten* in the chapter 'A reclaimed rubbish heap' she wrote:

> The crowning glory and wonder of the place is the garden, and the story of how that was made from waste ground used as a rubbish heap is typical of, and a good omen for, the whole undertaking. A little plot has been made up and a few seeds sown in the waste spaces of the Canongate, and it is to become a garden for work and play. Show people the way, and they will work at the garden themselves. (Hardy, 1913: 71)

First-hand experiences with and through nature, in the garden and the wild site of the forest school

As the sun shines on a beautiful autumnal morning and the children chatter busily and excitedly in the hall, collecting their belongings, the realisation of a new forest school programme begins.

Figure 5.2   Raphael toasting his marshmallow at the firepit

It is September and for the next six weeks, eight children and four adults will leave the centre to spend an uninterrupted period of time at our forest school site. In the centre our children can choose to be in the garden at any time of day. Our garden is small, but beautifully organised to support a wide range of learning experiences. It is a 'safe' environment that may limit risk-taking. The forest school environment supports risk-aware not risk-averse experiences for children (Figure 5.2). We believe that there will always be diverse definitions of what constitutes a forest school, but like all experiences offered to the children it should reflect the culture and community in which children live.

We wanted our forest school to provide an opportunity for children to become experienced risk assessors who are resilient and thoughtful about their own personal safety and who can make choices about what risks to take.

Adults role-model risk-aware behaviour, as Froebel augurs: 'The educator must also take into account the children's propensity to copy in their own lives the models set before them, and this is the greatest and most effective means of influencing them at this stage' (Lilley, 1967: 166).

Forest school enables children the experience of rich learning opportunities which are distinctive to the forest school experience. For example, the natural landscape offers children direct first-hand experiences of nature where they can know and come to understand the changing seasons. There are no toys.

The site itself fosters opportunities for folklore and inspiration for games of pigs and wolves and building houses to keep safe and hide from the wolves, or playing fairies and goblins, children have a wide range of opportunities to use their imaginations to convert features of the environment (see also the work of Hardy, 1912; McMillan, 1930).

> Play is the highest level of child development. It is the spontaneous expression of thought and feeling – an expression which his inner life requires. This is the meaning of the word play. It is the purest creation of the child's mind as it is also a pattern and copy of the natural life hidden in man and in all things. So it promotes enjoyment, satisfaction, serenity, constitutes the source of all that will benefit the child. (Froebel, in Lilley, 1967: 83)

Similar to our centre most early years environments have out-of-door spaces making it possible for the child to gain some knowledge of the natural world however, as mentioned above, the forest school experience can be contemplative and magical for children. In this 'space' the integrity of childhood is respected, uninterrupted (see Bowen, 1897); children can wallow, blossom and bloom away from the somewhat contained early years environment to a 'wild site' where children have more freedom in nature.

At forest school we return to the basics, learning how to be with ourselves and each other in a sometimes 'risky place', with its own challenges and delights. We have cook-outs and enjoy food together and do simple things. Commenting on just this, Liebschner shares Froebel's view:

> Froebel outlines in the Helba plan his belief that the acquisition of knowledge is the unification of the interaction between life and individual activity, between doing and thinking, representation and cognition, ability and understanding. All the education in these diverse situations should therefore be based on individual activity and self-representation. The doing together with the thinking was to be elevated to an educational aid and thus physical work was to be seen as part of education. (Liebschner, 1992: 17–19)

At forest school we, simply, do not have to write things down, but we might climb a tree, negotiate uneven ground, get stung by a nettle or get a bit wet and cold, or we might be too hot, or choose not to join in with our friends and choose instead to spend time in solitary contemplation. At forest school this is acceptable.

Small groups – belonging while being a separate and valued person

Our under 5s centre, like many other early years settings, is very busy and one of the most wonderful things about forest school is the opportunity to work with small groups of children. This offers teachers and practitioners the chance to really tune into children, as Kallalia claims: 'Educators who do not really see the child cannot fully bear pedagogical responsibilities' (2006: 124).

While early years teachers and practitioners support child-initiated play within their setting it can be more natural in forest school as children choose where they want to go and for how long, away from constant adult censure. Respect is given to time and uninterrupted play. This is the opposite of many aspects of a prescribed curriculum which tends to break down learning into predetermined subject areas with names such as 'language', 'mathematics' or 'science'. A more natural approach enables children to make more connections within their learning.

Just as Froebel studied plants and trees and became interested in natural growth this interest is reflected in the children's experiences as they do an investigation of the various tress, shrubs and flowering plants and animals on site. The children quickly learn and make connections between species; for example, bumblebees spend the long summer days collecting nectar from the wild flowers and in autumn berries feed the birds. For children, nature comes in many forms and the way in which children respond to nature can be very different from how an adult might react to nature. For example, at forest school the children explore nature in a way that is more 'natural' than do adults, they pause and wonder as they feel bumps on the trees; they look closely at the shape and texture of the leaves and are sensitively aware of the details in them. Then they see the similarities, unlike adults who classify almost without discovery, because they already know what the flower or shrub is. Froebel believed that through engaging with the world, understanding unfolds. Children, if given time, will use all their senses to make the discovery by comparing and contrasting. The names of species are not, at this stage, the most important thing for all children. But, because language develops so rapidly in the first five years, they learn the plant and tree names very easily if adults tell them what they are.

Nature offers healing for children living with concerns, or it simply provides an opportunity for solitude. It creates a space to be and to tune into the pace of nature. Froebel, too, turned to nature at an early age for solace and answers to his questions about life. It is no different for children today – children need nature, it is essential to their well-being.

In the city our lives can be very busy (see Tovey, 2007); however nature encourages us to slow down. Nature does not rush – trees grow in their own time, the flower blooms when it is ready. Children have more opportunities to relax in forest school, the child who leaves the building excited and chattering often returns more contemplative and peaceful.

The word 'respect' is very apparent in forest school; respect for the children who are with adults who trust that they can manage risk, risks such as stinging plants, or the use of sharp instruments; respect for the dangers inherent in fire or water; respect for nature and the forest environment.

As a result the children learn to care for nature and the environment, and learn to become experienced risk assessors who are resilient and thoughtful about their personal safety and who can make choices about what risks to take, for instance, helping children overcome what could be an overwhelming fear of getting lost is part of the forest school's emphasis on empowering children and developing their feelings of confidence and self-efficacy. At forest school we think about doing things slowly, one challenge at a time, developing the ability to manage one's own body in space, manage environmental features, loose material and other people. Every site will offer a variety of experiences to the child. These experiences will vary greatly. For example, a site that is in a large mature forest may have big climbing trees whereas reclaimed urban land may offer something quite different. Nevertheless, the experience will be educational and unique to each child.

What happens at forest school?

Our forest school experience is offered on four separate, but connected, six-week programmes. This means that all 32 children in the centre have the opportunity to attend.

In the hall the children are eagerly putting on appropriate clothing collecting their rucksacks. They demonstrate their inherent desire to be involved. They put on their rucksack, this item is very significant to the success of each child's forest school experience as it holds a self-chosen healthy snack and drink and additional clothing and footwear. The children take full responsibility for their rucksack from packing it to carrying it for the duration of time to and from the site.

As noted by Hardy: 'This is the age when instinct for activity and industry is strong' (1912: 48).

Preparation for forest school is important, the children need to consider what they need as there is no turning back. As a result children (quite quickly) learn what is essential in order to get the most from the experience. Furthermore, children share the responsibility of carrying any additional materials, such as litter pickers, rope and necessary materials to the site. Everyone takes responsibility in the true community spirit and a sense of unity and connectedness as the children learn to care for themselves, each other and the environment.

The child first needs to understand how they feel when stung and how to heal this, and then to think how other fellows will feel and help them. Using what they know to help each other. One example of this responsibility and community spirit is that the children quickly become their own first aiders. They learn where to look for a dock leaf to relieve the sting of the nettle, they also quickly help each other sourcing a leaf if they see a fellow adventurer being stung. As Bruce reminds us: 'Respecting other people is the foundation of moral and spiritual learning' (2004: 6).

Throughout the experience children are encouraged to become experienced risk assessors who are resilient and thoughtful about their personal safety, who can make choices about what risks to take.

The benefits of a Froebelian approach in working with nature – a modern approach

The 'wild site' is a wonderful learning resource. With all our forest school participants we are observing an increase in confidence, improved ability to work collaboratively and a greater respect for the environment.

We have discovered that children returning to the centre demonstrate improved concentration as they stay focused on tasks for extended periods of time and the level of interaction between them is beyond what they were previously capable of. Could this be because of greater intrinsic motivation? It seems that whatever their ages, abilities and interests, the children like getting dirty, muddy and stimulated, wearing clothes suitable for childhood.

The children are 'learning through' and not just 'learning about' things such as fires, shelters or climbing trees. On returning to the centre we witness children learning how to negotiate steps, ramps, climb up and over large pieces of equipment in the garden and use real tools at the woodwork table. As a consequence we observe them developing into competent, risk-aware rather than risk-averse learners

Benefits of free-flow play

There is a huge body of research (see Bruce, 1991, 2004) that demonstrates the vital importance to children of play as the most natural form of learning. The following extract from Hardy illustrates the importance of play in the lives of our children:

> The kindergarten discards the abstract learning and instruction which have no relation to the child's physical, mental or spiritual needs, and places him instead in a little world of action where he can develop his personality along the lines of his natural activities, his social life by contact with his peers. In his childhood there is only one true means of reaching self expression and that is play. (Hardy, 1913: 124–4).

Play that is freely chosen, often away from the adults' gaze, personally directed and intrinsically motivated is memorable, rich and often stays with us long into adult life as a vital sensory remembrance of our own childhood. Outdoors was often the place to be, and certainly not in an organised play space. Children work out their place in the world through play, they can be someone else, try out roles and imagine worlds for themselves: 'The fact remains that most of the best opportunities for achievement lie in the domain of free play with access to varied material' (McMillan, 1930: 80).

In our forest school sessions the best bits started to develop as we relaxed our hold on the planned experiences and started to allow free-flow play and child-initiated learning to emerge. As Bruce explains: 'In free-flow play, neither the child nor the adult knows where they will land up' (2004: 89).

Examples include children building a nest and pretending to be baby birds and then feeding each other with sticks as worms. One child spoke to the birds and the birds spoke back to him, as he prepared a trail of blueberries for them to eat – this resulted in wonderful connections being made the following week when he and a friend examined purple poo and deduced what had happened to the blueberries.

We realised quite early on that experiences planned by the adults, such as, 'hunt the ladybird' game or the forest school song, or simply the use of the magnifiers for observing tadpoles, would be quickly adopted by the children. Each experience however, became more complex and richer as they added to them. The ladybird game became a countdown for a rocket ship, which the children broke up and split into sections to hunt for an item that one child had hidden; the song became a sort of singing to the birds to get them to come down from the trees and join us, and the magnifying glasses were invaluable for looking at the patterns on the path, or identifying letters from children's names on the interpretation boards.

Benefits to children on self-esteem, emotional intelligence and behaviour

There is much discussion and research available about self-esteem and how it affects behaviour including whether it is low self-esteem or an over-inflated sense of self-worth which can cause many of the problems of modern life. In our view positive self-esteem could be defined as having a good sense of ourselves and our personal worth. The forest school experience provides an environment where children can develop confidence and competence in (somewhat more challenging) experiences. As Froebel discovered: 'They [children] do not want the easy occupations, but the hard work which demands strength and exertion …' (Lilley, 1967: 124).

Throughout the experience children's emotional intelligence is increased as they develop impulse control and persistent challenging experiences, such as tying the rope, whittling a stick or cooking a marshmallow. Children's confidence increased as they demonstrated a willingness to try new things. As Froebel warned: 'Teachers/practitioners should not speak so lightly and carelessly to the child and curb the flow of his strength and courage' (Lilley, 1967: 80).

They started noting whether something was a big deal or a little deal and this helped them cope with situations that may have been experienced as 'traumatic'.

Froebelian principles in this chapter

> There can be no happier people than those who believe in Froebel's principles – faith, in the universality and immutability of the law of love when it is applied intelligently, faith in childhood and its original purity, faith in humanity and its ultimate destiny. (Wiggin and Smith, 1896: 185)

Froebelian principles addressed:

- an ecological view of mankind in nature
- a holistic view of each child's development
- recognition of the child as part of a family and a community.

For us, this principle is concerned with the connections in nature, through community relations, involving children, family, staff members and the wider community.

Reflective question and practical action

- Consider how you connect with nature. How do you create and nurture a provocative environment for the children you work with?

Further reading

Bilton, H. (2002) *Outdoor Play in the Early Years*. London: Fulton.

Bowen, H.C. (1897) *Froebel and Education through Self-Activity*. New York: Charles Scribner.

Bruce, T. (2010) *Early Childhood: A Guide for Students*. 2nd edn. London: Sage Publications.

Bruhlmeier, A. (2010) *Head, Heart and Hand. Education in the Spirit of Pestalozzi*. Cambridge: Sophia Books.

Froebel, F. (1861) *The Pedagogics of the Kindergarten*. (Edited by W. Lange in 2001.) New York: D. Appleton.

Froebel, F. (1895) *The Mottoes and Commentaries of Friedrich Froebel's Mother Play*. H.R. Eliot and S.E. Blow (eds). New York: D. Appleton.

Isaacs, S. (1970) *Intellectual Growth in Young Children*. London: Routledge.

Knight, S. (2009) *Forest School and Outdoor Learning in the Early Years*. London: Sage Publications.

Lascarides, V.C and Blythe, H.F. (2000) *History of Early Childhood Education*. London: Falmer Press.

McMillan, M. (1930) *The Nursery School.* London: Dent.

Michaelis, E. and Keatley-Moore, H. (eds) (2010) *Froebel's Letters on the Kindergarten*. (First published in1891. Translated by Hermann Poesche in 1891.) Whitefish, MT: Kessinger.

Tovey, H (2007) *Playing Outdoors: Spaces and Places, Risks and Challenges.* Maidenhead: Open University Press.

Welter, V.M. (2002) *BIOPOLIS: Patrick Geddes the City of Life.* London: Massachusetts Institute of Technology.

Wiggin, K.D. and Smith, N.A. (1986) *Kindergarten Principles and Practice.* London: Gay and Bird.

CHAPTER 6

THE TIME-HONOURED FROEBELIAN TRADITION OF LEARNING OUT OF DOORS

JANE READ

This chapter focuses on Froebel's ideas about the role of outdoor environments and practice in his kindergarten for pre-school children in Thuringia, Prussia from 1837 up to his death in 1852. It explores how they were implemented in later settings for young children in the UK.

Observations of outdoor learning drawn from early education in the nineteenth century – Robert Owen (1771–1858), Samuel Wilderspin (1791–1866) and Friedrich Froebel (1782–1852)

Robert Owen

Robert Owen's monument in Kensal Green cemetery famously announces: 'He originated and organised infant schools'. Owen opened the first infant school in the UK at his New Lanark mills in 1816. In this school, key features included a focus on activity and play, the fostering of children's interest and curiosity and a strong emphasis on the natural world as a central topic for study and activities, including walks in the surrounding countryside. However it was another contemporary, Samuel Wilderspin, who effectively shaped the development of infant schools for working class children in the UK over the following decades. His design of a galleried infant schoolroom was adopted by the London School Board for its infant schools when it began to organise London's schools after 1870. The schoolroom could contain up to a hundred children. It was decorated with pictures and maps and there was a keyboard instrument for music.

Samuel Wilderspin

Wilderspin regarded a playground as essential for infant schools. Wilderspin saw the outdoor play space as providing opportunities for exercise but also for learning – as the children danced around the trees, each class having its own, they chanted the alphabet, recited arithmetic tables and sang hymns: 'Thus the children are gradually improved and delighted, for they call it play, and it matters little what they call it, as long as they are edified, exercised, pleased and made happy' (Wilderspin 1823, cited in McCann and Young, 1982: 24). Playground activities were also an opportunity for inculcating moral codes. The children learnt self-discipline – by learning to take turns on the maypole and wait in an orderly manner – and courage and dexterity in using the equipment. They were encouraged not to pick the fruit or flowers out of respect for the property of others.

Friedrich Froebel

Froebel's conception of the potential of the outdoor environment was very different. It was imbued with his philosophical beliefs and his visionary aspirations for children.

Froebelian practice with children and families: learning out of doors

The garden – a central part of the Froebelian kindergarten

In the kindergarten at Blankenburg the garden was a central feature of the kindergarten, with the surrounding countryside providing opportunities for direct observation of the natural world.. A contemporary print (Figure 6.1) shows that each child had their own plot to grow whatever they wished. It was

Figure 6.1 Blankenburg Garden

their responsibility to look after it, or not, the lesson being learnt if their plants died while the carefully tended plot of their neighbour flourished. If children had to share a plot, that provided an opportunity to learn to share and to work together. Children also worked with adults and the other children in the communal plots. Froebel deliberately placed the plots given to the children within the communal area to suggest to them the relationship between their individual plot and the area belonging to the community. For Froebel this was symbolic of the nurturing provided for each child by the kindergarten as well as for the child within the family, and the family within the community. Froebel also believed that as children watch plants grow they begin to understand something about the development of their own lives.

The countryside – beyond the garden

The children's outdoor experiences went far beyond the garden; Froebel took the children out into the surrounding countryside for play and for learning about the natural world in the surrounding fields, forests and orchards to extend their learning and to take part in cultivating crops: 'The child should study the basic natural products – stones, plants and animals; he should cultivate the soil, and work in field, garden and orchards.'

He took them to look at streams and to build dams to show them what happened to the flow of water, introducing children to cause and effect. Those working in the kindergarten had to be knowledgeable about nature and life in the immediate locality so they could introduce the children to them (Lilley, 1967: 118). Practical activities also took place – for example, the damming of streams which gave children a demonstration of the laws of cause and effect. Recognition of the child's need to be active was at the heart of the education Froebel proposed: 'Every being can only be developed through activity, doing and work ... can only become capable of understanding and reasoning through doing, work and thinking' (Froebel, cited in White, 1907: 16).

For Froebel the outdoor environment did not just provide opportunities for activity and doing and work, but also for thinking, for reflection on what was observed in the natural world. Activities in the outdoor environment aroused children's curiosity and encouraged problem-solving, persistence and respect for the natural world

Froebel said that active outdoor play was something that parents should also encourage in their young children.

> The great significance of childhood is that it is the period when the child develops his first connection with his environment and makes his first approach to an intelligible interpretation and grasp of its real nature ... Throughout childhood he should be allowed to maintain this connection with Nature and its phenomena as a focus of his life, and this is done mainly through the encouragement of his play ... (Froebel, in Lilley, 1967: 82–3)

Exploration and experimentation, adventure and challenge

Exploration and experimentation were driving forces in young children, and adults, in the kindergarten and in the home, needed to provide for them as they showed children that they can take control of materials and shape and form them as they wish. Froebel suggested parents should provide a garden for children at home:

> He is exploring everywhere and examining everything. He makes a little garden by his father's fence, maps out a river's course in the cart-track or ditch, studies the effects of the fall and pressure of water on his small water-wheel, or observes a piece of flat wood or bark as it floats on the water which he had dammed to form a pool ... he likes to be busy with plastic materials such as sand and clay which may be called a vital element for him. (Froebel, in Lilley, 1967: 127–8)

As in the kindergarten, it reinforced the message that their efforts would be rewarded as their plants grow and flourish. Their efforts would also attract animals which they could observe: 'he will see birds and butterflies and beetles coming nearby' (Froebel, in Lilley, 1967: 129)

Encouraging parents to involve their children in household tasks linking with nature

Parents should encourage children's active involvement in household activities as well as exploration of the natural world as it was closely linked to the development of language:

> He helps look after the animals, and make things for the house; he shares in the chopping, sawing and piling of the wood ... Question after question crowds out of his enquiring mind – how? why? when? what for? – and any passably satisfactory answer opens up a new world to him. He sees language as the instrument of communication for everything. (Froebel, in Lilley, 1967: 125)

Froebel says that adults who discourage children's involvement in activities may be doing great harm as physical activity was connected to creative expression (Froebel, in Lilley, 1967: 124). Instead, encouraging children's active involvement has positive outcomes, a child who 'never evades an obstacle or difficulty but looks for it and overcomes it'; in other words a child who developed persistence and mastery:

> 'Let it alone,' he will cry as his father goes to take a log out of his way, 'I'll get over it.' When he gets over it by himself, however difficult it may be, he is encouraged by the success and goes back to climb it again; soon he is jumping over it as if there were nothing in his way (Froebel, in Lilley, 1967: 124).

Such a child, Froebel argues, will express his energy 'in daring and adventure' as they explore: 'He climbs into caves and crevices, clambers up trees and hills, searches heights and depths, and roams through fields and forests' (Froebel, in Lilley, 1967: 126).

These experiences also help the child to understand the natural world: 'His aim is to enlarge his range of vision stage by stage ... He wants to seek out and find the undiscovered, see and know the unseen' (Froebel, in Lilley, 1967: 126).

In the course of their exploration the child will find all sorts of fascinating things: 'He brings back spoils of unfamiliar stones and plants, of creatures that live in the dark – worms, beetles, spiders, lizards.' Once again Froebel stresses the curiosity – the desire to know – which these activities arouse but he warns that adults needed to be cautious in their response to what children might bring to show them: 'What one must never do is to call out as he comes along, "Throw that horrid thing away" or, "Drop it, it will sting you." If the child takes notice he rejects something essential to himself' (Froebel, in Lilley, 1967: 127).

Children may learn things the adults do not know about the natural world

In the course of their exploration the child may well learn things which the adult may not know – things which are a source of wonder for the child and which will foster respect for the natural world: 'A little boy hardly six years old can tell you things about the wonderful organism and movement of a beetle which you have never noticed before' (Froebel, in Lilley, 1967: 127).

Froebel recognised that adults may be anxious about the risks in such play; they may fear the child will be reckless but he suggests that if a child is allowed to gradually develop their capacities then they will only attempt just a small step beyond what they have already achieved – it is only those who have been restrained who may try too much and 'run into unsuspected danger' (Froebel, in Lilley, 1967: 126–7).

So – adventure and challenge, curiosity, problem-solving, persistence, respect for the natural world – these were the lessons Froebel set out to convey. But what happened to Froebel's ideas when they arrived in the UK?

What happened to Froebel's ideas when they arrived in the UK in the second half of the nineteenth century?

In contrast to those children who enjoyed Froebel's kindergarten, the children of the working class in the UK attended the babies' classes and infants' schools which, from 1870, were the responsibility of the newly founded school boards, with attendance compulsory from the age of 5. The London School Board introduced aspects of kindergarten practice in the babies' classes and infants' schools. Froebel's Gifts and Occupations offered opportunities for 'manual training'. Froebel's wider vision was lost. There was no intention to foster his ambitious aspirations in the children of London's working class. The approach of the London School Board may well have been a pragmatic approach to a practical problem – how to provide an education for these children within financial limits acceptable to middle class ratepayers. Certainly the environments provided in London's infants' schools paid no regard to the importance placed by Froebel on free access to a variety of spaces.

The outdoor environment – tarmac

When Froebel's great-niece and pupil Henriette Schrader Breymann visited an infants' school in Stepney in July 1883, she wrote to a friend in Germany:

> I was much struck with the contrast between the arrangements made in Cambridge for the physical development of the students and the meagre provision made for the physical care of the young of the working classes. The poor little ones have not a small bit of earth where they can dig, or plant, not even a heap of sand, where they can make sand pies; the courtyard like the building was 'grey in grey', cold and hard and stony. (Schrader Breymann, in Lyschinska, 1922).

The Minutes of the School Management Committee's Sub-Committee on Kindergarten document the efforts of the Board's Superintendent of Method in Infants' Schools, Mary Lyschinka, to introduce gardening into the infant school curriculum. Her attempts to provide borders for the children to dig in were frustrated by caretakers and the school board's own works departments which refused to carry out the work. Complaints included the need to remove 'a nice Border of Shrubs' and the need for the care of plants during school holidays. Further, at one school it was noted that 'it has become necessary to tar-pave the borders provided in the playground for flowers and shrubs, as they have been trampled upon by the children, and the earth and mould carried into the school'. The Repairs Sub-Committee was more amenable and approved the suggestion of the Kindergarten Sub-Committee 'that permission may be given to the Infants' Teacher to make use of a small portion of the flower border in the playgrounds (say about 10 yards in length), for the use of teachers and children'. However photo-graphic evidence, for example, of the outdoor area of Southfields Infants' School in 1906, demonstrates the lack of imagination in the provision of garden areas in comparison with Froebel's vision at his Blankenburg kinder-garten. Schools were provided with a narrow strip along the edge of the tarmac playground which provided little opportunity for the individual and joint initiatives proposed by Froebel, which signified far more than a resource for nature study.

Dedicated Froebelian teachers – visits to the countryside

For most children in urban infants' schools, schooldays could hardly have been a joy, crushed into classrooms of up to 100 children. The youngest children in the babies' classes were frequently left in their rows at play-time as it took them so long to get in and out of the rows, particularly in winter when they needed coats and gloves. However some teachers who became familiar with Froebel's pedagogy began to introduce more exciting activities. Mrs Shaw, head teacher of Church Street Infants' School in Hackney, East London, applied to the Education Department in 1895 for permission to take the children to Epping Forest. The Department refused – so Mrs Shaw made the arrangements herself for an outing on a Saturday. She took 60 of her pupils to Epping, leaving the school at 9 a.m. and returning about 5 p.m. This was the first of a regular series of outings lasting throughout her time at Church Street. They collected nature study specimens for lessons but also for stocking the aquarium with snails, caddisflies, worms, and so on from the ponds. They also sent the children's work to the Nature Study Exhibition at the botanical gardens at Kew. This was a wonderful experience for these children; others had similar experiences in the voluntary settings which opened from 1900, the free kindergartens.

The free kindergartens and nursery schools – alternatives to gutter play

From 1900 free kindergartens opened in urban centres such as London, Birmingham and Edinburgh to give the poorest children the experience of a Froebelian kindergarten as an alternative to the cramped babies' classes. Part of the agenda of the free kindergartens, which were effectively the fore-runners of the nursery school, was to provide an alternative to gutter play, with the risks and dangers that attended it (Read, 2010). The prospectus for the Michaelis Free Kindergarten, founded 1908, described conditions in the streets as 'degraded and degrading': 'Indeed our horses and cattle are often better cared for than the young human lives which are growing up in stunted and depraved form in hundreds of our streets' (Michaelis Free Kindergarten Prospectus, 1908).

The second Annual Report of the Somers Town Nursery School, founded 1910, presented a typical argument in support of its work, expressing the dangers of unsupervised play:

> [W]hen one thinks of children spending the delicate and impressionable years of their lives in undesirable surroundings, untrained and uncared for, and probably acquiring degrading habits which tend to vice and crime, one can only be thankful for opportunities of helping even a few children in districts where such help is sorely needed. (Somers Town Nursery School. Annual Report, 1913: p. 6)

Looking back in 1933 the nursery schools' superintendent, Kathleen Stokes, recalled 'The first few children had literally to be picked from the gutter' (Stokes, 1933). Prior to opening the Michaelis Free Kindergarten in 1908, Esther Lawrence, principal of Froebel Educational Institute, echoed Froebel in proclaiming 'We must go into the streets and show the children how to play' (Reed, 1945: 6).

In Edinburgh, St Saviour's Child Garden opened off Canongate in 1906; its super-intendent, Lileen Hardy, recognised some benefits from street play but at a cost:

> Their [the children of the poor] only nursery is the street, and what they have there, though it may develop their wits, too often does so at the expense of finer qualities. Their imagination may be stimulated, but it is in an undesirable direction, and not beautifully, as a child's imagination should be stimulated. (Hardy, 1912: 85)

The integration of health and education – Froebelian pioneers in practice

The Froebel-influenced pioneers who opened these settings, of whom Margaret McMillan is probably the best known, argued that health and education – the ability to learn – were inextricably linked. McMillan, an active member of the Froebel Society for a number of years, drew heavily on Froebelian pedagogy. She provided an alternative vision to the infants' school – a 'school in the garden', a toddlers' camp which 'rings with laughter and the tripping of little feet' (McMillan, n.d.: 4). McMillan provided a rich garden experience for the children right in the middle of Deptford in the Rachel McMillan Open Air Nursery School in South East London. This nursery school for working class children was a 'provocative environment … where new chances are made possible' (McMillan, 1930: 78). Her environment was designed to meet the children's need for space: 'Children want space at all ages. But from the age of one to seven, space, that is ample space, is almost as much wanted as food and air' (McMillan, 1919: 10–11).

McMillan's nursery school and the free kindergartens stressed the benefits of the open air for the children's physical development and activities took place outdoors as much as possible, providing a rich sensory experience for exploration:

> Suppose you want to develop the touch sense! Lo! Here are a score of leaves, hairy sunflowers, crinkled primrose, glossy fuchsia, and the rose. Do you want to compare colours, to note tints and shades? Well, here is wealth a-plenty. The herb garden will offer more scents than anyone can put into a box, and a very little thought will make of every pathway a riot of opportunities. (McMillan, n.d.: 4, 5)

Experiences provided for children in the free kindergartens and nursery schools undoubtedly had a civilising agenda. Children swept and dusted and polished, learning about cleanliness and order. They played with each other, learning socialisation skills through sharing and taking turns. The open spaces of the street were now boundaried by the space limitations of the kindergartens and by circumstance: 'Whenever the weather is fine the children spend a great part of the day in the small garden' (Somers Town Nursery School, 2nd Annual Report, 1914: 2). The freedom they had enjoyed in street play gave way to permissions and allowances: '[T]he children are *allowed* to use the garden' (Michaelis Free Kindergarten Report, 1908: 110, emphasis added). Free play was partly replaced by organised games, based on Froebelian models. The found objects of the street gave way to manufactured materials for 'painting, drawing, building and other forms of handwork … suitable for the use of little children' (ibid.) – including, of course, the Froebel Gifts

Exploring the mud of the gutter and making mud pies was replaced by digging in the garden with the emphasis on horticulture, planting bulbs for example, and in the sandpit. Photographs showed this was not an activity which involved getting dirty!

There were also opportunities for creative and imaginative play, particularly with the junk materials, provided by fathers.

Figure 6.2   Nothing Hill Nursery School. Summer holiday, 1930s.

Annual holidays in the countryside

Free kindergartens and nursery schools began to extend the limited horizons of the children through long summer holidays in the country (Figure 6.2):

> [F]or six weeks in the year our children ... live for a short time a new life, in which they receive a totally new set of impressions, in which the sights and sounds and smells of the slums are replaced by those of the peaceful Sussex country ... they breathe the pure air blown from the sea, they run barefoot on soft grass, they wander at will in the sunshine and shade of garden and woods; becoming brown and strong and beautiful (Notting Hill Nursery School Annual Report, 1928: 14)

Annual reports of the holidays showed children's mixed reactions on seeing the sea for the first time: 'Tom Farley cried out, "My, ain't it big!" but little Billy Brackenbury was disappointed, and only said, "Is that all?"' (Anon, 1910: 17–18).

These annual holidays quickly became a tradition. While they undoubtedly provided opportunities for staff to work on language and manners and cleanliness, they provided children with joyful experiences of free play in wide open spaces, in line with Froebel's vision.

Froebelian principles in this chapter

- Learning through play in outdoor environments – Froebel advocates a wide range of learning experiences in outdoor environments, from digging in the garden at home or in the kindergarten, to play in public spaces of the town, to adventurous play in the countryside which challenges children but helps them learn safe boundaries.
- Child-centred learning – the focus is on letting children develop their own learning agenda, pursuing their own interests, and going at the pace suitable for them.
- Learning with supportive adults – adults, parents and practitioners, play a key role in supporting children's learning in outdoor environments. This might be providing resources (spaces to dig), joint activities (communal gardening, sharing household tasks) or stepping back when wanting to step in, allowing children to assess risk.
- Outdoor play stimulates wide learning – physical activity and exploration fosters curiosity and leads to those 'why' questions, so feeds into language learning.

Reflective questions and practical actions

- What do you think important to take forward into the future from the practice of previous historic times?
- What aspects of early childhood practice have changed little since the nineteenth century? Why do you think that is?
- What are you pleased has changed in early childhood practice today? Why?

Introductory reading

Brosterman, N. (1997) *Inventing Kindergarten.* London: Harry N. Abrams.

Further reading

Anon (1910) 'A fortnight's holiday spent at Westgate by forty-six children of the Michaelis Free Kindergarten', *The Link* (1): 16–18.

Brosterman, N. (1997) *Inventing Kindergarten.* London: Harry N. Abrams.

Froebel, F. Plan of an Institution for the Education of the Poor in the Canton of Berne, in I. Lilley (ed.) (1967) *Friedrich Froebel: A Selection from his Writings.* London: Cambridge University Press.

Hardy, L (1912) *Diary of a Free Kindergarten.* London: Gay & Hancock.

Liebschner, J. (1992) *A Child's Work: Freedom and Guidance in Froebel's Educational Theory and Practice.* Cambridge: Lutterworth.

Lilley, I. (ed.) (1967) *Friedrich Froebel: A Selection from his Writings.* London: Cambridge University Press.

Lyschinska, M.J. (1922) *Henriette Schrader Breymann. Life and Letters.* Unpublished and unpaginated translation in manuscript of M. J. Lyshinska, *Henriette Schrader Breymann. Ihr Leben.* Berlin and Leipzig: Walter de Gruyter.

McCann, P. and Young, F. A. (1982) *Samuel Wilderspin and the Infant School Movement.* London: Croom Helm.

McMillan, M. (1919) *The Nursery School.* London: Dent.

McMillan, M. (1930) *The Nursery School,* 2nd edn., London: Dent.

McMillan, M. (n.d.) *What the Open-Air Nursery School Is.* London: Labour Party.

Read, J. (2011) 'Gutter to garden: historical discourses of risk in interventions in working class children's street play', *Children and Society,* 25(6): 421–34.

Reed, L (1945) 'Miss Lawrence and the early days of the Notting Hill Nursery School', *The Link* (35): 6.

Stokes (1933) 'A short history of Somers Town Nursery School', *The Link* (23): 33–4.

White, J. (1907) *The Educational Ideas of Froebel.* London: University Tutorial Press.

Archive sources

Michaelis Free Kindergarten. *Annual Report 1928,* London.

Michaelis Free Kindergarten (1908) *Prospectus,* London.

Somers Town Nursery School. *Annual Report 1913, 1914,* London.

CHAPTER 7

FAMILY SONGS IN THE FROEBELIAN TRADITION

MAUREEN BAKER

Observations of Sylvie

Sylvie was born in September 2009 to Scottish parents. She has an older brother who is 13 years old and an extended Scottish family with whom she has close contact. In the nine months before she was born Sylvie was submerged in music. While in the womb she was already experiencing beat, rhythm and a variety of sounds and music as well as her mother's heartbeat. She experienced music sessions with her parents and their friends, her mother singing, her father playing the bodhran [an Irish hand-held drum] and her brother playing the bagpipes, keyboard and guitar.

Both of her parents were present to share her coming into the world. The moment she was born Sylvie was part of the culture that would form her childhood. Her parents will have their own ideas about parenting from their own upbringing, where they live and their life experiences.

> Babies are like the raw materials for a self. Each one comes with a genetic blue-print and a unique range of possibilities. There is a body programmed to develop in a certain way, but by no means on automatic programme. The baby human organism has various systems ready to go, but many more that are incomplete and will only develop in response to other human input. (Gerhardt, 2007: 18)

Lullabies

In the first few weeks of her life, Sylvie is soothed by her mother's voice and closeness. Her mother often hums tunes and sings her own versions of lulla-bies. Cass-Beggs (1969) points out that in every race and culture we will find mothers (and close members of the family) singing lullabies. These are often made up so that they meet the need of the baby in their family. This suggests that lullabies are fundamental to humanity.

Lullabies are sung predominantly for settling babies and putting them to sleep. Sylvie's mother sings spontaneously while she rocks and holds her closely. Parents instinctively rock babies as part of play or comfort. The repetitiveness of the lullaby comforts Sylvie, reminding her of her mother's heartbeat while in the womb. Research (Gerhardt, 2007; Goddard-Blyth, 2004) now shows that gentle rocking can help promote brain growth. Rocking stimulates the vestibular system in the inner ear. The vestibular system helps to keep the nervous system balanced.

Singing lullabies can also help strengthen the bond between parent and baby. The baby can benefit from hearing the familiar comforting voice. It is easy to see, when observing babies, that they prefer the voice of the mother or father to that of a stranger. This is especially noticeable during the first few week of a baby's life. Researchers observed that when the baby is listening intently to the voice of the parent while the parent is speaking to him, the baby's legs move in excitement (Malloch and Trevarthen, 2009).

Family voices are important

Sylvie becomes aware of the rhythm and intonation of her mother's voice and her mother gives her opportunities to engage in 'conversations'.

Sylvie's mother often massages her legs, arms and body, sometimes singing to her, making up songs including Sylvie's name. They share music times with Sylvie lying on her back. Her mother moves Sylvie's legs up and down to the beat of the music. Sylvie listens, smiles and moves her arms as her mother moves her legs. Her mother returns her smile. This chimes with Froebel's instruction to parents and grandparents, and mothers in particular. Froebel emphasised the fact that doing things for themselves leads even very young children to self-knowledge. He called this the 'self-activity' of the child.

Eye-to-eye contact becomes important (Figure 7.1). Malloch and Trevarthen (2009) comment on the way that babies seem to be fascinated by human faces,

Figure 7.1   Building Relationships: Sylvie gazes at her mother who is quietly singing to her

so much so that they will draw comfort from the face of someone who gives them loving care. The affection in the person's eyes and the sound of their loving voice have this effect.

When the situation is right, Trevarthen (2004) emphasises that newborn babies can be very good at imitating the expressions of people. They read very precisely the emotions in a face or voice. They hear and are able to identify subtle differences when a different language is spoken. He points out that by 2 months of age, what he calls proto-conversations are developing. This means that babies co-ordinate their expressions and gestures with a sympathetic parent, and make great efforts to, as it were, 'talk'.

Sylvie becomes familiar with other family members. She looks intently at her brother's mouth as he makes different sounds. This game lasts for more than 10 minutes. Sylvie and her brother are in tune with each other. Her brother finishes the game by ruffling his head on Sylvie's tummy and she laughs. He laughs too.

Singing with Sylvie – diversity in languages

Sylvie's great grandmother sings rhymes in the Shetland tongue. Sylvie, 3 months old, looks intently at her great grandmother. Other family members join in. Sylvie's gaze moves from person to person and she moves her hands while they sing.

Sylvie's grandmother sings traditional rhymes in Scots language.

Sylvie is already forming relationships with people who recognise her needs, enjoy being with her and respond to her. They become significant adults in Sylvie's life. Bruce (2004) emphasises that people, babies and adults need other people. She suggests that we both influence and are influenced by others in the ways we feel, think, develop ideas, move and relate to people. It is just as important to pay attention to these sociocultural aspects of development as to study the brain's development.

Bath-times and song, splash and movement

Sylvie and her mother have already built a trusting relationship and both enjoy bath-time, a time to develop Sylvie's senses through playful rhymes

Initially, Sylvie kicks both feet up and down, splashing water out of her small bath. After about 5 minutes her mother shows her a duck and sings 'This little duck went swimming one day'. Sylvie stops splashing and focuses on the duck. She moves her gaze to her mother and smiles. Her smile elicits a smile from her mother. The pace of the rhyme is set by Sylvie. When she stretches out her hand, her mother gives her the duck. Sylvie immediately puts it in her mouth and explores the duck by sucking and licking it. Bath-time lasts 24 minutes. It is another intimate time for Sylvie and her mother to share.

Sylvie is doing what babies of her age often do, exploring the plastic duck first by touch, followed quickly by sucking and licking. The activity of one sense can lead to the heightening of another sense. The reaction of hearing on sight will be evident to anyone who will notice how much more strongly visible things appeal to the baby when interpreted by word and tone. On the other hand, vision reacts upon and incites to activity the sense of hearing. Often, when a baby sees and feels she also tries to taste and everything her hands can grasp is promptly directed to her mouth.

The importance of 'tummy times'

Sylvie loves lying on her tummy on her floor mat and stares for long periods of time at the details of a variety of farm animals. Rhymes and songs are sung about the various animals. Sylvie's grandmother sings in Scots 'Katie Beardie had a coo'. Sylvie moves her head from side to side. She moves her arms and legs as she engages in the play. Sylvie's mother sings to Sylvie every day when she is on her mat.

Froebel (Lilley, 1967) says: Therefore dear mother let it be your aim to train the senses that you shall at the same time, cultivate the heart and intellect; and in order that you may realise this aim, make clear to yourself the correlative truths that the soul activity of your child manifests itself in his sense activity, and that through sense-activity he struggles towards the soul of things. (*The Mottoes and Commentories of Friedrich Froebel's Mother Play*: 6, 78.)

More recently, Penny Greenland (Bruce, 2010: Ch. 16) emphasises the importance of the senses and movement in the education of very young children.

Touching and hugging

Sylvie experiences a wide variety of rhymes, songs and music. She enjoys the closeness of her mother as they share a tickling rhyme 'This little piggie' (Figure 7.2). Her mother touches her toes one by one as she recites the rhyme. Sylvie watches her mother intently and laughs when she gets tickled at the end of the rhyme.

Babies love to touch and hug their toes. Froebel called this an aspect of unity, which involved the way that different body parts relate to each other and co-ordinate. In this he anticipated more recent studies of the brain.

Figure 7.2   Developing Language and Body Awareness Sylvie and her mother are both deeply involved as they share the rhyme 'This little piggie'

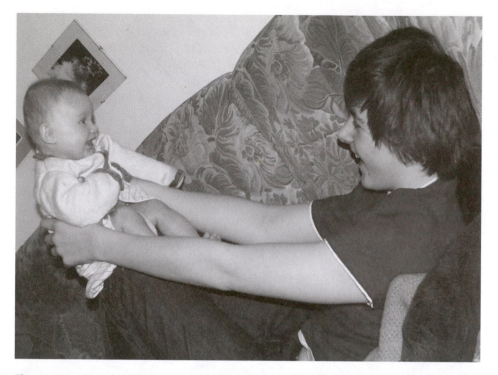

Figure 7.3 Communication: Sylvie and her brother are looking intently at each other and enjoying 'The Volcano' a made-up song

Sylvie's brother made up a sliding song called 'The Volcano'. Sylvie sits high on her brother's knees, the top of the volcano (Figure 7.3). He sings the volcano song. As the song progresses, Sylvie anticipates the sliding down movement. Her brother holds her and slides her down the volcano. She squeals with delight. The song is repeated again and again. There is a the feeling of slight shock of falling as she slides down but it is experienced in the safety of the song

Froebel (1967) writes directly to parents suggesting that it is through what he terms 'this falling or slipping play', with the baby supported, loved and protected by the parent's care, that the baby increases both in strength and consciousness of strength.

Sylvie's first experience in her bouncer is made enjoyable by her mother's presence. She maintains eye contact as she is supported to sit upright. This is a new experience for her. Her mother makes up words to a rhyme as she bounces. Sylvie moves her arms and legs causing her to twirl around. She laughs and smiles every time she turns to her mother. The experience is repeated later with her father.

Sylvie is building a positive image of herself and has a sense of belonging from the pleasurable shared experience. The beginnings of emotional understanding are formed when babies get reactions and responses from people around them. Stern called this attunement. He believed and thought that babies can withdraw from situations if people do not tune into their needs and they find it too difficult to get responses. However, a sense of belonging is central to the principles of diversity (Bruce et al., 2010).

Sylvie is not even 6 months old and has a wealth of songs, music and rhyme. She experienced her first ceilidh at 4 months old, watching the Highland dancers, moving her gaze from one to the other while moving her own arms, head and legs. She was taken in a baby sling to concerts by her parents. She has heard her brother play bagpipes on a variety of occasions

Sylvie and Bookstart

At age 4 months Sylvie received her first Bookstart bag from the library. A bag containing a CD, board books, notes for parents and other information.

Sylvie already enjoys sharing books with adults and is very relaxed sharing one of the Bookstart books with her grandmother. Sylvie looks at the front cover, smiles, becomes very animated and begins babbling. Is it the colour, the illustrations, the print or her already developing love of books, or the shared experience that induces this reaction? Does she recognise a bear, a rabbit or a duck from the toys she is already familiar with or has seen in real life?

She holds the book independently for 8 minutes, lets it go and moves her hands all over the cover making excited utterances. She becomes totally absorbed for 7 more minutes. She is given the opportunity to wallow and enjoy only the cover. Maybe page one tomorrow? The rhyme in the book will become familiar at a later stage.

Later Sylvie enjoys the book by herself, holding the book and looking at one of the pages.

Already Sylvie has so many experiences to build on.

Sylvie enjoys peek-a-boo games

At 9 months old Sylvie enjoys peek-a-boo games (Figure 7.4).

She now understands that if an object/person moves out of her line of vision and hides behind a cushion cover, it might return. She leans over, moving her arms in anticipation of the surprise return. Sylvie takes control of the game. She covers her own face with the cushion cover and listens to the rhyme. Her mother uses language rhythmically and introduces a made-up song, changes the tone of her voice and pauses to give Sylvie time to react. Sylvie squeals with excitement when she reveals her face. She repeats this game again and again for 12 minutes. Sylvie becomes aware of her grandmother taking photographs and looks and laughs towards her, extending the activity to a wider group. She smiles, makes her own utterances and continues for a further 8 minutes. She finishes the game by giving the cushion cover to her mother.

Figure 7.4   A made-up song is being sung to Sylvie as she plays peek-a-boo with her mother

Froebel might see peek-a-boo games as satisfying hide and seek and meeting the craving for recognition.

> Babies can only learn the spoken languages they hear. They can only play in the way people show them. Experience influences the forms that language or play will take. (Bruce, 2002: 12)

Music

Sylvie, 5 months old, is listening to her brother playing the penny whistle. Her eyes are fixed on his face, she is seriously intent and concentrating. After about 8 minutes her mother hands Sylvie a penny whistle sideways, she turns it round and sucks the blowing end. The game continues for about 4 minutes. She then puts down the penny whistle and laughs and 'chats' to her brother. He continues playing. Both appear to be enjoying the shared experience.

Sylvie and her brother are sharing a musical time together. Her brother, 13 years old, is playing the ukelele. Sylvie's gaze moves from the ukelele to her brother. She listens seriously and intently, sometimes moving her legs. Her brother is aware of her presence and her gaze and plays on for 4 minutes. Both are content in each other's company.

Sharing experiences that both find pleasurable

Sylvie has often seen blackbirds in her grandmother's garden. She has heard the birds sing, watched the blackbird flying from feeder to trees, jumping on the grass, feeding on worms, splashing in the bird bath and sitting on the wall.

Outdoors she enjoys the rhyme 'two little dickie birds'. The words are changed to 'two little blackbirds sitting on granny's wall'.

Sylvie is happy to see the two forefingers representing the birds flying away. She copies her grandmother putting her hands over her shoulders and waits in anticipation for the rhyme to beckon the birds back

Sylvie and her grandmother often walk around the garden, looking at and listening to the blackbirds. Her grandmother whistles, Sylvie laughs and touches her grandmother's lips. She tries to whistle, pursing her lips and making a 'phew, phew' sound as she blows. (This is a similar mouth movement that she makes when she hears the bagpipes.)

Sylvie is 10 months old and can now crawl and pull herself up. She draws on past enjoyable experiences and crawls over to her brother when he is playing the guitar. He continues playing as she pulls herself up towards the guitar and touches the strings. Sylvie moves her body from side to side and 'sings' in a high-pitched voice. The shared experience lasts more than 10 minutes. Her brother offers her the opportunity to 'play' by herself. She looks at him he nods says 'you play' and she plucks the strings, looks at her brother and smiles. He returns her smile and the playing continues.

Sylvie can now make choices independently. She often chooses to look at her *Katie's Coo, Scots Rhymes for Wee Folk* (2009) book. She is able to hold the board book and turn the pages. She looks with intent at each page as she works her way through the book. She offers the book to her mother who sits on the floor to share the book with her. The first rhyme they enjoy is a favourite tickling rhyme 'Roon aboot, Roon aboot'.

Sylvie and her mother interact for about 6 minutes, repeating the rhyme several times. Sylvie moves her hand round and round as her mother says the first line, laughs and tightens her arms towards her body in anticipation of the tickling. The book lies on the floor and although it prompted the rhyme it is not referred to.

Sylvie and her mother use the book for the the next rhyme 'I've a kistie I've a creel'. Her mother says the rhyme while pointing at the illustrations. She repeats the rhyme more slowly. This time Sylvie points to the illustrations. The last line reads 'Yin, twa, three, four' Sylvie lifts her hands and touches the fingers of her left hand with the fingers of her right hand as if counting her fingers (Figure 7.5).

Figure 7.5 Spontaneity: Sylvie's mother reads a familiar rhyme and Sylvie responds spontaneously

Sylvie has experienced a range of lullabies, tickling, clapping, bouncing rhymes and play songs

Sylvie has also been exposed to a wide range of music and she now turns her head when she hears music. She moves her hands, legs, head and body as she listens. She has handled a variety of instruments and can bang, hit, tap, shake, scrape, scratch and blow. She also enjoys plucking and twanging. She has shared these experiences with her immediate and extended family, and with family friends who have become significant people with whom she has positive relationships

Perhaps she will attend rhyme time sessions in the local library or any of the many more organised events for under 3s in the city where she lives. Her parents may or may not choose to let her experience a pre-school setting where trained staff will recognise and build on her already rich experiences.

Sylvie celebrates her first birthday with her parents, 'mummu and daddee', her brother 'buva' and her grandmother, 'gaga'. She had watched her mother bake her birthday cake repeating 'pat a cake' rhyme several times during the experience. She worked alongside her mother, smelling, licking, biting and patting her own piece of dough. A few days later she attempted to recite the rhyme while patting the dough and deliberately and delicately poking holes in it with her index finger. Her mother varied the activity by clapping and patting Sylvie's hands with her own hands.

Practical work with children and Families – Froebel's Mother Songs today

Froebel realised that his Gifts did not cater for the earliest stages of a child's development, the time when the child experiences the world primarily through movements, limbs and senses. This led to him compiling the Mother Song book in 1844. The complete title of the Mother Song Book reads: *'Come let us live with our children, Mother Songs as well as songs for games with body and limbs and senses. For the early and uniting care of Childhood'* – *A Family Book by Friedrich Froebel.* Froebel calls it a family book. He describes it as containing poems and pictures whose aim is the noble nurture of child life and adopts as its motto the saying of Schiller 'Deep meaning oft lies in childish play'. (Froebel, *Pedagogics of the Kindergarten*, 2001: 6.)

In the original volume there are 207 pages, 50 with pictures for the child, 50 pages with a poem for the mother and a poem for the child. The remaining 107 pages are addressed the mother alone and in part to the mother and father.

Froebel (1844: 1) had no doubt of the book's significance: 'I have recorded the most important aspects of my educational theory in this book; it is the starting point for an education based on nature, for it shows the way. How the germinal buds of human potentials have to be nourished and supported if they are to develop healthy and completely.'

The songs in the book were for babies, toddlers and young children and relevant to the culture and times the children lived in. However, a few of the rhymes, such as 'Pat-a-cake' are shared by mothers and babies today. On the whole they are usually now performed with less detail, especially the detail of finger play. One of the purposes of the book was to develop a child's 'body, limbs and senses' in various finger plays and games with mother. Froebel referred to the mother/baby relationship when he said: 'She feels the dignity and importance of what she is doing, guided by her maternal instincts. Her loyal and loving heart is full of the call "Come let us live with our children"' Froebel, in Lilley, 1967.

Much research has been carried out by neuroscientists, psychologists and others since Froebel's time. Colwyn Trevarthen, at Edinburgh University, has carried out extensive research by observing mothers and babies. In 1998 he referred to the high-pitched voice used by a mother when communicating with her baby as 'motherese' which is biologically right for babies and toddlers. His research (Malloch and Trevarthen, 2009) focuses on how musicality starts in relationships between infants and adults. Trevarthen finds that adults and babies are predispositioned to speak and coo at each other in rhymes and melodies right from birth and that this interaction affects emotional and cognitive growth.

Trevarthen suggests that the mother's smiles and songs are dances of 'reciprocal communication'. This is based on physical closeness, and is critical for mother/baby bonding and the child's developing feelings of security and self-worth, known as attachment (Bruce et al., 2010; Grenier, in Bruce, 2010: Ch. 12).

Music is powerful in its relationship to mental and physical processes. Adults play vocal games with babies such as 'Round and round the garden' and 'Roon aboot, roon aboot runs the wee moose'. These movement activities contribute to a baby's sense of belonging to their family, community and culture. The Scottish culture has a rich heritage and tradition of music and rhyme which is a powerful means of passing on heritage and culture. Many of the rhymes have been sung by generations of parents and children. They keep the past alive and form part of the child's identity

Nowadays, life moves at a very fast pace. Parents have choices. They can sit their baby in a bouncy chair and try to amuse her with colourful toys, sit her in front of the television to watch bright colours and fast movements or they can talk and sing to her. Television cannot interact or give a sense of security and love. Parents and babies develop positive relationships by talking, singing, listening, touching, imitating and turn-talking. Active participation using songs and rhymes can be a source of fun, enjoyment and learning for both parent and baby

Froebelian principles in this chapter

- Recognition of the uniqueness of each child's capacity and potential.
- A holistic view of each child's development.
- Recognition of the importance of play in a child's development and learning.
- An ecological view of humankind in the natural world.
- Recognition of the integrity of childhood in its own right.
- Recognition of the child as part of a family in a community.

The above Froebelian principles can be identified in Sylvie's music song rhyme experiences. In the first year of her life Sylvie has been recognised as part of her immediate and extended family. Positive, supportive relationships have been nurtured through sharing music, songs and rhymes that are appropriate for her stage of development.

Her family shares her capacity for enjoying and participating in music, song and rhyme. They give her opportunities to take the lead and introduce new songs and rhymes when appropriate. Rhymes are used in a variety of situations helping Sylvie to develop a deeper understanding of the world around her.

'Five Little Ducks' is sung at bath-time while Sylvie plays with her plastic ducks. It is sung outdoors when feeding the ducks and when visiting the farm. The rhyme is sung again when Sylvie is looking at pictures of ducks in her books and when she plays with small world ducks.

'What the child imitates,' says Froebel, 'he begins to understand. Let him represent the flying of birds and he enters partially into the world of birds. Let him imitate the rapid motion of fishes in the water and his sympathy of fishes is quickened. Let him reproduce the activities of farmer, miller and baker, and his eyes open to the meaning of their work. In one word let him reflect in his play the varied aspects of life and his thought will begin to grapple with their significance.'

Playing with voice sounds, rhymes and songs is given high priority for Sylvie. It is a means of communicating, expressing and sharing enjoyment, heightening body awareness, developing physical movement. Sylvie's holistic development benefits from the wide range of musical activities she engages in daily.

Sylvie's time as a baby is being recognised as a unique stage in her development. She has significant adults who are tuned into her needs and who enjoy playing and learning with her.

Many babies depend on care settings for the experiences Sylvie has had at home and it is important that adults in such settings reflect on their practice to ensure that babies in their care are exposed to an abundance of rich experiences which ensure the babies in their care progress in their development and learning.

Practitioners should continually reflect on their practice and be aware of the importance of music song and rhyme and how these are offered to each baby/child in their setting.

Reflective questions and practical actions

- How can music, song and rhyme help build relationships with babies/children?
- What status does music, song and rhyme have in your planned daily provision?
- How does your setting plan music activities for individual babies/children to show progression?
- How does spontaneous music, song and rhyme feature in all areas of your setting, including outdoors?
- How does music, song and rhyme impact on other areas of a baby/child's development?
- How do you work with parents to share a baby/child's musical interests?
- Examine your current practice in music, song and rhyme.
- Ensure that babies/children in your care daily experience a wide range of music, song and rhyme.
- Foster links with parents that share their baby/child's musical enjoyment and progress.

'No child should be deprived of the joy of singing', Christopher Bell, Artistic Director of The National Youth Choir of Scotland

Indeed man's whole development requires that his surroundings speak to him clearly in their outward appearance and that in childhood he is able to see and understand what it is they are saying. So in her words and songs the mother tries to express these and bring the life of his environment closer to him so that he will feel and find himself. (Froebel, in Lilley, 1967: 105)

Introductory reading

Bruce, T. (ed.) (2010) *Early Childhood: A Student Guide*. 2nd edn. London: Sage Publications.

Bruce, T., Meggitt, C. and Grenier, J. (2010) *Childcare and Education*. 5th edn. London: Hodder.

Cass-Beggs, B. and Cass-Beggs (1986) M. *Folk Lullabies* Harlow: Pearson Education.

Cass-Beggs, B. (1980) *Your Baby needs Music*. Harlow: Pearson Education.

Geoghegan, L. (2002) *Singing Games and Rhymes for Tiny Tots*. Glasgow: The National Youth Choir, Scotland.

McVicar, E. (2007) *Doh Ray Me When Ah wis Wee: Scots Children's Songs and Rhymes*. Edinburgh: Birlinn.

Books for Babies (2009) *Katie's Coo: Scots Rhymes for Wee Folk*. Edinburgh: Itchy Coo.

Further reading

Bruce, T. (2002) *Learning through Play: Babies, Toddlers and the Foundation Stage*. London: Hodder & Stoughton.

Bruce, T. (2004) *Developing Learning in Early Education*. London: Paul Chapman Publishing.

Bruce, T. (2011a) *Early Childhood Education*. 4th edn. London: Hodder Arnold.

Bruce, T. (2011b) *Learning through Play*. 2nd edn. London: Hodder & Stoughton.

Bruce, T. and Spratt J. (2011) *Essentials of Literacy from 0–7*. 2nd edn. London: Sage.

Froebel, F. (1885) *The Mottoes and Commentaries of Friedrich Froebel's Mother Play*. H.R. Eliot and S.E. Blow (eds). New York: D. Appleton.

Froebel, F. (1895) *The Mottoes and Commentaries of Friedrich Froebel's Mother Play*. H.R. Eliot and S.E. Blow (eds) in 2004. Honolulu University Press.

Gerhardt, S. (2007) *Why Love Matters*. London: Routledge.

Gopnik, A., Meltzoff, A. and Kuhl, P. (1999) *How Babies Think*. London: Weidenfeld & Nicoloson.

Greenland, P. (2006) 'Physical development', in T. Bruce (ed.) *Early Childhood: A Guide for Students*. London: Sage Publications.

Liebschner, J. (1992) *A Child's Work: Freedom and Guidance in Froebel's Educational Theory and Practice*. Cambridge: Lutterworth Press.

Lilley, I. (1967) *Friedrich Froebel*: Cambridge: Cambridge University Press.

Malloch, S. and Trevarthen, C. (2009) *Communicative Musicality: Exploring the Basis of Human Companionship*. Oxford: Oxford University Press.

Ouvry, M. (2004) *Sounds like Playing*. London: British Association for Early Childhood Education.

Poulson, E., Roeske, C. (music) (1921) *Finger Plays for Nursery and Kindergarten*. Norwood, MA: Norwood Press. (Originally printed in Boston, MA in 1893 by Lothrop, Lee and Shephard Co.)

Prufen, J. (1927) *Friedrich Froebel*. Leipzig: Mutter und Koselieder.

Woodhead, M., Faulkner, D. and Littleton, K. (1998) *Cultural Worlds of Early Childhood*. Maidenhead: Open University Press.

CHAPTER 8

THE IMPORTANCE OF HAND AND FINGER RHYMES: A FROEBELIAN APPROACH TO EARLY LITERACY

JENNY SPRATT

It is always important to bear in mind the good practice from the past, and to take it forward in updated forms. Looking at the work of Froebelian pioneers in the early kindergartens, favourite books of mine are by Elizabeth Harrison, *A Study of Child and Nature from the Kindergarten Standpoint* ([1893]/1895) and Emilie Poulson ([1893]/1992). I was lucky to purchase a copy of Poulson's work (verses, music and illustrations). These books reflect Froebel's last work, the Mother Songs (1844). Froebel pioneered the thinking that children can learn a huge amount about communication, language and literacy when they share songs and finger rhymes with their parents.

Historically, in the Mother Songs, Froebel refers to finger games and Emilie Poulson (interpreting his work in 1893), refers to 'finger Plays'. This is different from the modern interpretations of finger rhymes. Finger rhymes were originally literally play using the fingers. Froebel developed the rhymes in early nineteenth century to:

- develop the relationship between mother (or father, grandparent) and child within the family context
- introduce the child to the whole of a concept before it is broken into parts, enabling young children to see the unity of the whole and to show the parts of it within the whole
- introduce a physical aspect to the game, where the whole person is involved in the exercise – the senses and the mind as well as the limbs.

Froebel wrote the songs to be used originally by the family at home, but they were later used by the female kindergarten teacher. The following observations of William show his journey from birth to his first engagement with finger rhymes, using a Froebelian approach.

Observations of William

Sounds

Even in the first month of being born, babies react to sounds around them, whether they are loud and soft sounds, particular music, or the voice of parents and close family. This will be important later when they learn to read and write. Literacy is rooted in being increasingly aware of sounds and being able to discriminate between similar sounds, where they come from and how they are made.

Hands

William is just born. He is already moving his fingers, in response to the voice of his grandmother. As a newborn baby, William is very short-sighted and can only focus at a distance of 12–17 centimetres from his face. He is probably not aware that his hands are part of himself. He is fascinated by the movement of his own hands, which takes place within a limited visual field.

William has the classic 'Asymmetrical Tonic Neck Reflex' (ATNR). This is described by Sally Goddard Blythe in her book, *The Well-Balanced Child* (Goddard Blyth, 2004: 4). It means that William's hand and head are all locked together into a single movement. This movement places the hand in a new position from which it can be viewed. This helps William to extend his focusing distance from near point to arm's length. William's hands are clenched during this action.

At two and a half months after his birth, William's hand comes into contact with a variety of objects that his parents begin to offer him to hold. This contact (hand with object) helps him to see how far the object is from his hand. Movement, vision and touch all combine to sow the early seeds for William's later ability to focus his eyes at different distances. This is the first and earliest kind of hand/eye/movement co-ordination.

Sight

There are other ways of extending the range of gaze, such as hanging mobiles above William's pram. The mobile needs to be within his best range of vision (as we saw at the beginning of the chapter). William reaches out his hand, swiping with his tight fists. Gradually his hands will open out, and he will be able to grab the mobile. It is interesting that his favourite song at the library 'Bookbugs' group is, 'Eyes, Nose, Cheeky, Cheeky Chin'. This involves his mother touching the relevant part of his body while singing the rhyme.

At around three months William's hands begin to open from tight little fists. Trevarthen (2004: 14) says: 'Objects are now discovered at an accelerating pace, by the combined application of hands, eyes, ears and mouth to pick up useful information.'

Once William is sitting, crawling (and walking), it becomes even more important to be facing him when he is pushed in a pram or buggy. His parents will have 'increased eye contact and more opportunities to stimulate talking at an important stage in the development of a child's language abilities' (Gadhuk, 2011).

Sitting

Sitting is a landmark for William and any baby. There is a huge variation in the age at which this happens, but William is 6 months old when he begins to sit unaided. He experiments with reaching for objects in his treasure basket which is placed in front of him. There is plenty of toppling over as he works out how to balance around his midline, but this does not put him off! Babies are biologically driven 'to seek out and create the experiences they need' (Greenland, 2006: 163–4).

As William changes from being a toppling over easily sitter into a confident and more stable sitter, his hand movements develop rapidly. His hands are free, and his thumb is the only digit on his hand that has the freedom to swivel or rotate. His thumb is unique in that all of its movements can take place independently of any of the fingers.

Sitting on the floor, William is grounded and balanced. This will be important, as we shall see, when engaging in finger rhymes.

William explores what his hands will do, clenched, gripping and holding, spreading out and rotating his thumb, but he also continues to develop hand contact with objects, just as he did when lying down, before he could sit or crawl. Now he widens the range of objects he can hold. He can use a 'cradle grip' (with his hands spread out around the object) to hold still larger objects,

Figure 8.1   Cradled object

so that he can examine and explore them (Figure 8.1). He still clasps smaller objects in either hand, usually putting them in his mouth for added information of their properties, but the cradle clasp means that he can use both hands together in a co-ordinated way. In his high chair he can hold a spoon and balance the upturned yoghurt pot on the top. Using hands can be creative!

Crawling

Sally Goddard Blyth (2004: 6) suggests that during the first 9–12 months William will acquire thousands of new movement patterns and movement abilities. At the same time as these movements are being learnt, William is replicating the brain development of evolutionary ancestors, from the aqueous environment of the womb where movements are fish-like in character to crawling on the belly which is sometimes seen as having parallels with reptilian ancestors.

Once William is crawling on his hands and knees, as many mammals do, he has open hands as he moves about, because his hands are spread out as he makes contact with the ground. This is important for fine motor skills and writing later on. Developing eye tracking means he is able to look easily around the room. When a child crawls, two important things happen to the hand:

- The hand is spread out.
- Leaning on the floor puts pressure on the palm of the hand, which the child feels.

Crawling is important for William's future learning because it 'supports a strong sense of the centre of the body while in motion. It is the first time that children experience balancing at the same time' (Greenland, in Bruce and Spratt, 2011: 65). When William learns how to crawl, it is the first time that he is able to look from side to side as he travels along. This will be important when he learns to read later on.

The community and the unique child – connections

William goes to a singing group with his parents usually, but his grandparents take him when they visit the family. William sits on his grandmother's knee. He engages with the finger rhyme, looking at the singer/leader of the group, and feeling his hands go up in the air as his grandmother moves his arms up in the air, like the leader. The Froebelian concept of unity is here. He is part of a whole community of singers and movers. Interconnection is at the heart of this.

William also enjoys books, and points at objects in them, expecting Grandad to name them for him. William is progressing well along his journey to literacy.

A Froebelian approach to practical work with children and families

Early childhood practice in most settings today seems to have lost the essentials of what is important in finger rhymes according to Froebel's vision of how they can contribute to a child's education and home life. Liebschner (1992: 115) suggests that during the 1920s the Mother Songs were interpreted in ways which made them become cosy nursery rhymes, with the emphasis on keeping children happy. They were used to occupy and distract children rather than to educate them. This contrasts with Froebel's thinking, which was more in line with modern findings from the neurosciences. Blakemore and Frith (2005) suggest that each time the same finger is stimulated the connections between the activated network of neurons become stronger and stronger.

Mollenhauer (1991: 287) describes the sensations that the child might experience when engaging in finger rhymes during a close physical relationship with the parent/carer:

> While it moves its fingers, the child can feel the play of muscles and sinews perhaps as far as the elbows. We may assume that the child's attention is firmly fixed on itself, or at least on its own body. The inner sensations of the child's body, hands, eyes and ears all share in an all-consuming awareness of the mother's words and gestures.

Froebel's Mother Songs show a progression in the rhymes, which develop from finger rhymes to travelling or journeying plays to representational plays and running plays. The distinctions between different kinds of action songs has been lost, and it is now rare to find practitioners who take time to reflect on and make use of this aspect of traditional Froebelian practice.

Taking forward Froebelian practice in relation to finger rhymes and action songs in today's context

It is always wise before embarking on the introduction of any changes in practice, to research what is actually happening in schools and other settings. We therefore decided to undertake a survey in the English local authority in which I work, in order to audit the use of finger rhymes in their current early childhood practice. The following questions were asked:

- Which finger rhymes do you use most regularly in your setting?
- Which nursery rhymes do you use most regularly in your setting?

Observations of practice were also made by the advisory team, and these raised further questions. Finger rhymes were not being distinguished from action songs and nursery rhymes. But did they need to be?

Many children were observed with clenched hands, rather than spread, relaxed hands. Penny Greenland (2010) of Jabadao (the Centre for Developmental Movement Practice) suggests that children who have clenched hands have probably not had sufficient experience of crawling when they were babies. There is a link here with Elizabeth Harrison (1895: 166): 'The clenched hands denote the struggle within, and great artists often use them as the only marked sign of the inward turmoil which the calm face and strong will are determined to conceal. The open and extended palm indicates entire freedom from deceit or concealment.'

At this time the local authority was invited to take part in the English National Programme on Early Reading. We decided to develop our work on finger rhymes, action songs and nursery rhymes, linking to Froebelian practices in updated form.

We identified (Spratt, 2007) the range of skills that the child was observed using during different rhyme activities, suggesting that some skills are generic across all kinds of rhyme. These are auditory, perception, rhythm, imitation of sound, pitch, intonation, memory and close relationship with peers. The level and focus of other skills appeared to vary according to the type of rhyme.

Finger rhymes

Finger rhymes provided a fine focus to skills used by children in the reading process that action songs did not provide, such as close relationship with the adult supporting the child in the visual tracking of the hand, leading to symbolic representation of the hand and finger, which later, in reading, will become the symbolic representation of a symbol for a sound (the grapho-phonic link).

Observations suggested that activities like finger rhymes have become, according to Nylan et al. (2008: 73) 'ritualised exercises' and 'suggesting that if adults do not listen to the language of the hands, they are depriving themselves of a valuable window into children's thinking and learning'.

In our survey we found the most used finger rhymes used by practitioners were:

1 Tommy Thumb
2 1, 2, 3, 4, 5 once I caught a fish alive
3 Two little dicky birds
4 Five little men in a flying saucer
5 Five current buns
6 Incy Wincy Spider
7 Five little monkeys jumping on the bed
8 Twinkle, twinkle, little star
9 Five little ducks
10 Five fat sausages.

But are these finger rhymes? According to the traditional Froebelian approach, only two qualify as finger rhymes. These are 'Tommy Thumb', and 'Incy Wincy Spider', although Twinkle, twinkle has recently developed into one in the way it is sung.

'Tommy Thumb' uses the fingers , first by naming them as parts of the hand (thumb and so on), and second by giving each finger a character. In other words, it has the possibility of transforming the fingers and so encouraging the child to move from the literal (naming parts of the hand) to the symbolic (meeting Toby Tall and Peter Pointer).

In the same spirit, in 'Incy Wincy Spider' the fingers move in a definite way, but this movement pattern becomes the spider climbing the drainpipe.

In 'Twinkle twinkle' the hand is clenched and spread, clenched and spread, a physical sequence of movement, which becomes symbolic of the twinkling of the star:

> What the child imitates he begins to understand. Let him represent the flying of birds and he enters partially into the life of birds. Let him imitate the rapid motion of fishes in the water and his sympathy with fishes is quickened. Let him reproduce the activities of farmer, miller and baker, and his eyes open to the meaning of their work. In one word let him reflect in his play the varied aspects of life and his thought will begin to grapple with their significance. (Froebel, in Poulson, 1983: Preface)

We had, in our survey, asked 10 parents in every setting (schools and private settings, voluntary and independent sectors) to answer these questions:

• Do you sing nursery rhymes and songs at home with your child?
• If you do, which do you sing?

We did not specify finger rhymes, just nursery rhymes as we used this as a generic term that we thought would be more familiar to families.

The most sung nursery rhymes by parents with their children at home were:

1   Twinkle twinkle
2   Baa baa black sheep
3   Wheels on the bus
4   Row, row, row your boat
5   Wind the bobbin up.

It is interesting that parents identified two nursery rhymes and then three action songs. Many parents mentioned popular culture songs, and songs from television programmes.

We used the information from the survey in developing our thoughts about introducing an approach to finger rhymes, nursery rhymes and action songs which had more inner cohesion, and found ourselves drawing heavily on the thinking (but not the songs) of Friedrich Froebel.

Finger rhymes were introduced using three stages.

Stage 1

Introduce rhymes that just use the hand so that children experience unity within the whole. The rhymes involve the whole hand and all ten fingers, opening and shutting. Example: 'Open, shut them' (for more detail see Bruce and Spratt, 2011).

Kuhlman and Schweinhart (1999) suggest that the whole of motor development exhibits sequentially. Children learn first to sit, crawl, walk and run. They distinguish between the locomotive and non-locomotive movements in sequences. Finger rhymes use the non-locomotive movements. Weikart and Carlton (in Kuhlman and Scweinhart, 1999) suggest these progress from simple to more complex movements:

1   Both hands perform the same movement at the same time.
2   One hand performs the movement alone.
3   Hands alternate to perform the movement.

Stage 1 is important because it opens up the opportunities for children to know themselves as physical beings, and that your finger is always your finger, no matter how you move it about. Children need to sit on the floor (not on chairs), so that they feel comfortable, grounded and balanced. This enables them to move the top part of their bodies with the bottom part feeling safe and secure.

It is a physical skill to focus closely on the fingers and then to be able to focus beyond. The finger rhymes encouraged this changing of focus in helpful ways.

During this stage, we observed children extending the palm of their hand more often than before, and hands were less often clenched. Children were encouraged to be aware of the sensations in their hands as they stretched or squeezed them. Their visual gaze of the hands was enhanced (Figure 8.2). Children were getting to know themselves as physical beings, and they enjoyed the anticipation in the finger rhymes

Stage 2

Introduce rhymes that use the fingers to represent parts of the body, again supporting the child's developing understanding of interconnectedness as part of unity – the fingers are part of the hand. Different fingers are isolated during the finger rhyme. Example: Tommy Thumb.

By pretending the fingers are something else, children's thinking gains a symbolic life and dimension. Children experience drama, and they develop their own personal style. They begin to become proficient in linking beat and rhythm to phonic sounds, appreciating anticipation and variety.

Children can change 'identity' of the fingers, using their voices and movements and shapes of fingers to represent different things. Their fingers can become what they want them to be.

We observed that children were able to isolate the different fingers and talk about the position of their fingers more readily. Their visual tracking improved and there was an increase in vocabulary. The imagination developed with more symbolic representations, and children anticipated the words and finger movements.

Stage 3

Here we find rhymes that use the fingers to represent objects from nature or community or food. Example: Two little dicky birds.

In the first part of the chapter, we met William, from a few days after his birth until the approach of his first birthday. From birth he has been using his hands and developing control of them. He enjoys 'baby songs' and before he

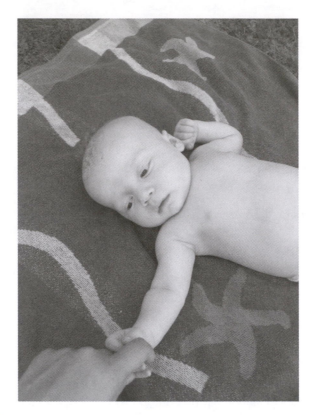

Figure 8.2   The gaze

is 1 year old, already begins to use his whole hand in stage 1 of the finger rhymes. It is important to consider the development of babies in this way, so that practitioners who work with babies understand their possibilities and respect the depth and fulfilment of learning they can enjoy if given the opportunities.

It is the sensation of touch in the different movements, supported by the 'looking' that is important. The children refer to 'Ruby Ring' as the 'tricky one', but they can now hold 'Ruby Ring' up straight.

During stage 3 the finger rhymes link gross and fine motor movements. The gaze is extended beyond the fingers. Children use their fingers as symbols, and the finger rhymes begin to link with stories. Children develop a sense of pantomime and drama.

Mollenhauer (1991: 296) suggests that 'the child learns to devote attention to the field of eye and hand and to localise the hand as the all-important medium in his field between the far-reaching eye and the immediacy of the body' (see Figure 8.2 above). This visual fine focusing is a prerequisite for reading, and Clay (1986) suggests that children arrive in school with far less skill in analysing two-dimensional space as:

In pre-school, children are constantly looking upon a wide view, viewing much and seeing little. This causes some children to observe far less than they could. Seeing must go beyond just looking. It must become a systematic search for precise information and an ability to structure a mental representation of the forms that are seen. School work (reading) requires near print vision and the development of new and precise focussing skills.

Froebelian principles in this chapter

The Froebelian principle permeating this chapter is that of interconnectedness.

- Conscious unity of all things was central to Froebel's philosophy and in the Mother Songs he provided mothers at home and, later, teachers in the kindergarten with unity. This is in relation to the external world through the senses (taste, smell and sound), unity within the family and unity in nature (Brosterman, 1997: 32).
- In the chapter we see two examples of unity: William as a baby within the unity of the family, and of children within the unity of the kindergarten. We also have examples of how young children experience the unity of their whole body first before they can break down the use of the various parts. We see William developing from birth and being able to co-ordinate and use his hands, at first separately, but later, once he is sitting, to use both hands together to investigate and manipulate an object. This replicates the intention of Froebel's first Gift – to enable the baby to investigate the properties of the unity of the ball. We also see the children in kindergarten enjoying finger rhymes with their teacher, starting with rhymes that use the whole hand and progressing to finger rhymes that use individual fingers – introducing the parts.
- In both examples we see unity with nature – William is in a buggy facing his parents so that they can talk to him about nature and the kindergarten children using their fingers to symbolise animals and birds.

Reflective questions and practical actions

- When do you sing finger rhymes with the children you work/live with?
- How do you introduce a new finger rhyme to the children? Do you give enough repetition? Do you give time to practise hand and finger movements? Do you explain the story of the rhyme? Do you encourage change of visual gaze from close to more distant?
- How do you differentiate between finger rhymes and action songs? Do you make a distinction between hand/finger movement rather than whole body movement?
- What skills do you think children use when they sing finger rhymes?

Introductory reading

Bruce, T. and Spratt, J. (2011) *Essentials of Literacy from 0–7: A Whole-Child Approach to Communication, Language and Literacy.* 2nd edn. London: Sage Publications.

Whitehead, M. (2010) *Language and Literacy in the Early Years 0–7:* 4th edn. London: Sage Publications.

Further reading

Goouch, K. (2007) 'Parents' voices: a conversation with parents of pre-school children', in K. Goouch and A. Lambirth (eds) *Understanding Phonics and the Teaching of Reading: Critical Perspectives.* Maidenhead: Open University Press.

Goswami, U.(2007) 'Learning to read across languages: the role of phonics and synthetic phonics', in K. Goouch and A. Lambirth (eds) *Understanding Phonics and the Teaching of Reading: Critical Perspectives.* Maidenhead: Open University Press/McGraw-Hill.

Mollenhauer, K. (1991) 'Finger play: a pedagogical reflection', *Phenomenology and Pedagogy*, 9: 286–300.

Nylan, B., Ferris, J. and Dunn, L. (2008) 'Mindful hands, gestures as language: listening to children', *Early Years: An International Journal of Research and Development*, 28(1): 73–80.

Poulson, E., music by Roeske, C. (1921) *Finger Plays for Nursery and Kindergarten.* Norwood, MA: Norwood Press. (Originally printed in Boston, MA in 1893 by Lothrop, Lee and Shepard Co.)

Whitehead, M. (2009) *Supporting Language and Literacy Development in the Early Years.* 2nd edn. Maidenhead: Open University Press/McGraw-Hill.

CHAPTER 9

FROEBEL'S MOTHER SONGS TODAY

MARJORIE OUVRY

Observation of a child

Henry (three and a half) comes across the well-organised inside music area in the nursery. A set of graded chime bars is arranged on a stand with the highest bar at the top. This attracts Henry's attention and he reaches for two beaters – one for each hand. A practitioner quietly watches what he is doing as he listens to how the force of his beater makes a dull thud on one bar but a differently pitched sound on one higher up. She is not going to interrupt him by showing him that if he bounces the beater it makes a different sound. But she notes the possibility for later. He then strikes a tambour and, alternating, he hits the lowest chime bar and the tambour, the next chime bar and the tambour and so on right up to the topmost chime bar. He has composed! The practitioner remarks on his composition, 'Henry, I heard two different sounds as you gave the chime bar a turn and then the tambour a turn, the sound of the tambour, "bang", and the sound of the chime bar, "tang" – bang, tang, bang, tang, bang, tang, right up to the top'. The practitioner asks if she can try to imitate what Henry has just done and the composer agrees! She realises that what might have been perceived as random noise if she had not been watching was in fact a patterned and rhythmic composition which required co-ordination and planning, concentration and accessibility.

Practical work with children – Where are we now and how did we get there?

People tend to think that some of us are born musical and some of us just aren't! It is the luck of the draw if you can sing or play an instrument well. But there is an increasing body of research refuting this notion (Harrison, 2007, cites Trevarthen, 1989, Papousek, 1994 and Mithen, 2005).

We are all born with an amazing capacity to make music. Music is and has been throughout our evolution an essential means of human expression and communication. Otherwise it would have just died out. So it would seem terribly wasteful if this fundamental form of exchange of ideas is not promoted in the education and childcare systems right from the start. How many people have there been who have successfully conveyed their thoughts and emotions, revealed to others events in their lives that mattered to them, through this heightened form of expression? How many have been frustrated because they couldn't? If music is an innate ability, have many of us been thwarted in nurturing it and have been 'put off' music at an early age by the way in which it is offered in the educational arena? What is happening in early years that is encouraging or discouraging the progress of this art? It used to be the mainstay of early education.

The prioritising of music and movement in nursery and infant education to foster and encourage innate musicality has a long tradition dating back to before Friedrich Froebel (1782–1852). But it was he who highlighted the importance of singing and finger rhymes and games in infancy. He called them Mother Songs.

Coming forward into the 1950s, for example, when I was an infant in school, we had 'music and movement' regularly as a radio broadcast. Victoria Wood (Wood, 1983) wrote a comic song about a cynical and disaffected lad forced to endure the schools broadcast.

It's bad enough at school without the wireless

We have it almost every afternoon

Its something called **music and movement** where you run about to a tune

I wouldn't mind if it was cops and robbers

But the lady tells you what you have to do

Be as small as a mouse, be as tall as a house

I'm knackered and it's only half past two!

The difference was that unlike the lad in the song who hates music and movement, I just loved to escape from the classroom boredom and listen to the lady on the radio. Back then it was an integrated and essential part of what was offered to children.

Sadly this legacy which came down to infant and nursery teachers from Froebel is in decline if not altogether gone. Alas, practitioners are not taught the history of infant and nursery education and do not know that there is an honourable tradition that they would do well to follow.

The decline in music education in the early years

As I visited students in a variety of early years settings in my job as a nursery nurse course tutor in the late 1970s and early 1980s, I was saddened by the lack of music in the settings. The practitioners seemed to know very few songs and tolerated practice for music teaching that they would not have allowed in other areas of the curriculum. Music almost invariably happened in large groups. There was no evidence of music play or independent exploration of music and few well-planned music areas. Unappealing heaps of musical instruments were brought out from time to time for all the children to bang or shake excitedly, eliciting pained looks on some children's faces, and there were always one or two who covered their ears to soften the noise which seemed to hurt their delicate hearing. Could this approach be the start of disaffection with music in education?

From the surveys that I undertook recently into music teaching in the early years, sadly not much has changed. Although there is much more music available for children to hear, electronically, the important element of the personal transmission is missing. Does this matter? I think it does and neuroscience backs this up. Brains like to imitate! Some neuroscientists believe that the muscles that are employed by the adult to sing to the child are mirrored in the child's throat, causing empathy of expression. It is important to keep music live and part of the relationship between adult, practitioner or parent, and the child.

What has happened to music in the early years?

I have already alluded to the cultural changes that make music into a second-hand experience transmitted by electronic devices. But there have also been changes in teacher training. Since the mid-1970s the concept of infant and nursery education as separate specialisations in teacher training has become blurred. The generic teacher training means that subjects (mathematics, science, literacy, and so on) dominate the teacher training curriculum. It seems to be a lottery as to whether teachers in training will encounter lecturers who know about child development and early years pedagogy, or whether they will see music teaching in their early years placement that is appropriate to that stage of development. My research (Ouvry, 2003) found that teachers are confused and lacking in confidence when it comes to early years music and this lack of confidence insidiously leads to bad practice. It leads to a lot of sitting in whole groups: 'The longer you keep children sitting the less attentive they become. Increasing the number of adult-directed tasks at the expense of play leads to the early signs of ADHD, especially in boys' (Pellegrini, 1998).

Imagine that you are 4 or 5 years old and you are taken to the hall, along with the other 29 in your class. Sitting in a big circle, you see a shaker start its journey from hand to hand around the circle as a song is sung. The song stops and you find that you are holding the shaker which you have rarely seen before. You are asked to do something with the shaker. You shake it! The teacher says, 'Very good.' The song starts again and the shaker moves on. That is your experience of music for a week.

The reception class experience is the most important time in the whole of the child's school life. (Harvard Research quoted in *TES* Friday Aug. 10 2010). The impression that children gain then about their school learning ability stays with them throughout their schooling and beyond.

Connecting with Froebel Mother Songs

I have discussed what might have led to the decline in appropriate teaching of music in early childhood settings:

* cultural changes leading to lack of knowledge of traditional songs and music and singing heard but without the necessity of active and physical involvement
* lack of appropriate early years music teaching in teacher education and other practitioner training
* consequent lack of practitioner confidence leading to inappropriate practice
* marginalisation of music teaching.

How can revisiting Froebelian philosophy help us move forward into good practice?

Studying Froebel can help us to see that children's requirements do not change with time. What Pestalozzi, Froebel, Steiner and many great education philosophers found out, that children needed, by observing them intelligently and sensitively, is now endorsed by our modern educationists, psychologists and neuroscientists. Babies and young children need to sing and be sung to.

Why *Mother* songs? The foetus in the womb hears and feels the vibrations of the mother singing. It is the *voice* of the mother that provides an acoustic connection between life before and after the birth. We know now that songs get the infant ear and brain ready for the sounds of speech and thinking in words. The voice of the mother and father as they sing to their child fuels far more than just the baby's hearing.

Froebel realised the incredible opportunity young mothers were missing in the development of their children's capacities for learning. Much of his work was in developing songs, hand activities and games for mothers to play with their children.

As an example of finger-play songs we can use one from our own time and one from Froebel's book of Mother Songs (1843):

Tommy Thumb

Tommy Thumb, Tommy Thumb, where are you? Here I am; here I am, how do you do?

Peter Pointer, Peter Pointer, where are you? Here I am; here I am, how do you do?

Toby Tall, Toby Tall where are you? Here I am; here I am, how do you do?

Ruby Ring, Ruby Ring where are you? Here I am; here I am, how do you do?

Baby Small, Baby Small where are you? Here I am; here I am, how do you do?

Now we can look at a similar song from Froebel's Mother Songs in translation.

This little thumb

What's this? what's this? what's this?

It is a little thumb round. It looks just like a plum round.

And this? and this? and this? This little finger points the place,

And straight it is, yet full of grace;

And this? and this? and this? This finger doth the longest show,

And makes the middle of the row,

And this? and this? and this?

This one the golden ring shall wear, and like the gold is pure and fair.

And this? and this? and this? This finger is the least of all,

And just completes the number small,

Oh yes, it is, it is!

And though these little gifts Have each a part to fill,

They're all together bound, And governed by one will.

And though these little gifts Have each a part to fill,

They're all together bound, And governed by one will.

'This little thumb'(Figure 9.1) is similar in intention to 'Tommy thumb, where are you?' Both songs feature the baby's fingers but Froebel's song is a much more advanced tune with far greater pitch ranges, from middle C to the F sharp more than an octave away! A child cannot sing that range but can internalise it and can join in with the 'What's this?' as the adult sings and draws attention to each of the fingers in turn. It has a new tune variation for each finger, is much longer and is generally much more complex. Froebel highlighted the notion of holistic learning and it is interesting to see that the last line of the song talks about how everything is united and bound together.

Music specialists get concerned about giving children songs in the right pitch for their supposedly high little voices or teaching songs that are just the right difficulty. Colwyn Trevarthen (in a Scottish Teachers TV interview) said that the difficulty of the song (or the dialogue with a child) is not the issue but rather that the child is in the company of a singer or a communicator and the relationship is the key factor. We must revitalise live singing and finger rhymes

This Little Thumb

What's this? what's this? what's this?
It is a little thumb round. It looks just like
  a plum round.
And this? and this? and this? This little
  finger points the place,
And straight it is, yet full of grace;
And this? and this? and this? This finger
  doth the longest show,
And makes the middle of the row,
And this? and this? and this?
This one the golden ring shall wear, and
  like the gold is pure and fair.
And this? and this? and this? This finger
  is the least of all,
And just completes the number small,
Oh yes, it is, it is!
And though these little gifts Have each
  a part to fill,
They're all together bound, And
  governed by one will.
And though these little gifts Have each
  a part to fill,
They're all together bound, And
  governed by one will.

Figure 9.1   This Little Thumb

in our settings, and for that to happen practioners need to learn and get to know, by heart if possible, lots of songs. In Froebel's book of Mother Songs are songs for all occasions from mowing grass to windy days.

Singing everywhere – connecting with home and community

In my in-service courses I give a little 'test' to practitioners and ask them to list at least three songs in each category from the following list:

- finger songs and games
- action rhymes – songs and games that need space (songs for outdoors)
- clapping and stamping songs
- rocking and lullaby songs
- songs with the child's name in them
- songs about (1) animals, (2) birds, and (3) farms and (4) dinosaurs
- songs about people who help us, doctors, firefighters, and so on
- made up songs to help children tidy up and remember routines
- songs about plants and planting
- songs about different weathers, snow, rain, wind, and so on.
- songs to support schemas, rotation, enveloping, transporting, and so on
- songs for Christmas.

I want practitioners to realise just how many songs they know already but because they don't plan to weave music into everything that they are doing with children as they interact in play and exploration situations, they forget to sing them at the relevant times, or they might feel self-conscious. Practitioners need to make an effort to learn songs in order for these songs to become so ingrained that they do not have to think about which songs to sing and where. I would like to see collections of songs and rhymes as a part of the assignments of early years teachers and other practitioners in training. One way to be reminded of songs and games is to have laminated sheets with lists of the current songs being learnt and to put up these sheets at the music areas inside and outside too. But not only at music areas; songs can also be sung in the home corner, and so a list of relevant songs could be there too. For example, lullabies beside the dolls' beds in the home corner or washing songs (Rub-a-dub-dub, dirty socks in a tub) behind the sink in the kitchen area of the home corner. In my book, *Sounds like Playing* (Ouvry, 2003), there is a CD with songs which connect with what children do in the nursery or reception class (Primary 1 in Scotland) – a song to sing at the sand and water tray, when building with crates or blocks, or in the home corner, and so on.

> A practitioner had co-constructed a 'car' out of chairs, tyres and blocks and the children sitting in the car started on their journey.
>
> 'Has this car got a radio or CD player?' asked the practitioner. That provocation was enough for the children to start singing and revealing to the practitioner their repertoire of songs.

Reminding ourselves of the songs we know and learning new ones is as important as keeping the sand topped up or making sure all the dolls have clothes that fit. It is part of what we do as practitioners. We have no excuse for not taking time to learn songs as the Internet is full of nursery songs (for example, at bbc.co.uk/nursery songs and rhymes) and every songbook nowadays comes with a CD (for example, those published by A&C Black) that we can listen to and learn from. At first, if you lack confidence, you can sing along to the CD, but nothing beats the eye and voice contact that you have with the children when you are singing off by heart. When our voice is leading the singing then we do not have to go at the pace of the CD. We can vary our pace, speeding up and slowing down to accommodate the difficult bits.

> Today the most urgent need in education is that the school should be united with the life of home and family.
>
> (Froebel, 1826)

If we do not work closely with parents we put all the responsibility of making the connections onto the child and that is not fair!

Making the connections for the children we work with applies to music too. We teach children songs and it is important that the parent is encouraged to sing these songs at home. A few strategies for involving parents in singing are listed below.

- Type the words of the songs you are teaching to the children onto individual slips of paper (type once then copy and paste *ad infinitum* and cut into slips!). Parents can help themselves to a slip. The container on the notice board can be labelled 'Song of the week'.
- Have a sing-along at the end of the session when parents/carers are collecting the children.
- Have home-made books of songs in the waiting area.
- Make a CD of your songs and give (or sell) it to parents, for example, Christmas songs, nursery rhymes, songs about the themes you are exploring.
- Accompany the CD with a book made by the children who have illustrated the songs.
- Find out which parents play instruments and ask them to come into the setting and play their instrument to the children. If you work in a school,

Figure 9.2   Chelsea Pensioner

older children may like to come into your classroom or outside area to 'perform' to a little group of younger children who will be an adoring and uncritical audience.

- Find out what music is happening in the community. One school near army barracks invited the band to come to play to the children, another invited a local bagpiper and yet another invited a Chelsea Pensioner to play his regimental drum (Figure 9.2).

Connecting music education with Froebelian philosophy

Play in young children is the characteristic activity of childhood; it is the highest phase of child development at this period; for it is self-active representation of the inner from inner necessity and impulse. Play is the purest, most spiritual activity of man at this stage and, at the same time typical of human life as a whole – of the inner hidden natural life in man and all things. It gives therefore joy, freedom, contentment, inner and outer rest, peace with the world. It holds the source of all that is good. (Froebel, 1826: 30)

Observation and play – starting from what we know already

Young babies realise they have an effect on the world through the first rattles they play with. They grasp the rattle, it makes a noise, they repeat the action, they know about shaking! Of course, young children know about banging and hitting, scraping, blowing and twanging from the interaction with objects in the world. It may be the stick that they scrape along the railings or the tin that they bash with the spoon. No one has 'taught' them but they *learn* through the exploration and *get to know* through play.

The introduction of percussive and tuned instruments helps children move on in their exploration of sound and music areas, for child-initiated composition can provoke further discovery.

It is really important that the music areas, established inside and out, have some sort of organisation and purpose that can make sense to the children. A box of assorted drums and shakers randomly left for children to use is far less likely to focus children's attention than a well-organised area. A few carefully selected instruments that are attractively placed on corresponding photographs or silhouettes, and labelled, will aid experimentation much more than an arbitrary assortment of grubby plastic toy instruments. For example, the music area may for a time have instruments selected for the way they produce sound, two cane shakers (to shake), two wooden agogos (to scrape or hit) and a set of chime bars (to hit). There can be a laminated notice on the music area which aids the exploration.

In our music area are instruments to shake, scrape and hit

Although there are whole-group times where one or two children can augment the songs by the use of instruments with purpose and direction from the adult, at the music area all sorts of ways of producing sound can be explored and observed, and child-initiated compositions can be developed with the interested adult.

A practitioner wanted advice from me. Her nursery had a very good music area but the children did not use it. I asked her to monitor how often the staff went near it! We need to build time into our planning to support children's ideas or they get stuck and lose interest. As adults with more experience, we have to show a genuine interest in what children are doing and model musical behaviour for them to imitate or aspire to. When we observe children's seemingly random exploration of instruments we find there are method, organisation and pattern.

How can we support children as they play instruments in the music areas indoors and out and with small groups or individual children?

- By listening and responding to what children say and do as they play.
- By modelling (playing one of the instruments ourselves).
- By singing as they accompany us or vice versa.
- By copying what a child does. (Adult says, 'Am I playing the same pattern you are playing?')

It is important if you want to organise the music-making in your setting to take an inventory of your instruments and only retain quality instruments. You may find that you are lacking a range of instruments from each category, that is, banging, scraping, shaking or tuned percussion such as chime bars, glockenspiel or xylophone. In which case, only buy good quality natural instruments from a music instrument catalogue. Do not buy plastic toys as instruments for your setting. They are not respectful to children, they do not make sounds that are satisfying and they break easily and cause frustration. Organise your music areas well and put only a few instruments out at a time.

Making instruments with the children can virtually cover the whole curriculum! Home-made instruments are also very useful in filling any gaps in the set of instruments. For example, twanging instruments can be made by stretching elastic bands over a strong box and will stimulate lots of experimentation in creating tuned sounds from children and adults! Blowing instruments are the cheapest of all! We all carry them with us in our throats; they are our voices which, if used, will meet all the criteria of the elements of music. If you want to highlight the voice then have Kazoos or swanee whistles for children to blow. The benefits of the voice and singing cannot be over estimated.

Opposites

Everything and every being comes to be known only as it is connected with the opposite of its kind and as its unity, its agreement with its opposite is discovered. Froebel, F. (1896) *Education by Development*.

Each of the elements of music has its opposite.

The opposite of Loud	is	Quiet	(Volume-dynamic)
The opposite of High	is	Low	(Pitch)
The opposite of Fast	is	Slow	(Speed or tempo)
The opposite of Long	is	Short	(Duration)
The opposite of Hard	is	Soft	(Timbre or quality)
The opposite of Thick	is	Thin	(Texture)
The opposite of Silence	is	Noise	

The composer plays around with these elements to make a pattern which includes the pulse or beat and rhythm.

As we listen and observe our children playing with instruments we notice that they rarely use these elements randomly, but rather with real intention. It is at this point that we can intervene if appropriate and extend or reflect on the child's composition. This is illustrated in the observation at the top of this chapter.

Look out for composers!

We can help children by talking in a musically appropriate way when we observe them playing with the instruments. For example, we can *describe* what the child is doing and *reflect* back on her activity: 'You are scraping the guiro very fast.' This comment provokes the possibility of the opposite as does the comment, 'Listen, I am playing quietly.'

We can *discuss* with the child how his composition makes us feel and engage the emotional response, 'That sound makes me feel happy' thus triggering in the child the chance that music could make you feel the opposite. 'How does that sound make you feel?' Or we can *remind* the child that sounds can imitate, 'That sounds like leaves rustling to me, what about you?'

It is in engaging in a musical conversation with children that we can show how seriously we take their journeys of discovery. We can comment descriptively, or comment on the technique they are using, on the ability of music to imitate or affect our emotions. The sounds that the children make on the instruments can be used in enhancing story-telling. A child using the chime bars to make the ding-dong doorbell can make all the difference to a story such as *So Much* (Cooke, 1994). There are countless stories that come alive when instruments are used as sound pictures.

What is the musical home life of our children like? Its culture is bound to have a huge influence on them. Music in the home involves technologies, with children singing along to favourite songs on radio, television and CDs. Toys are bought that play tunes electronically when a button is pushed and catchy advertising jingles are remembered, for example, 'Go Compare!' It has been argued (Young, 2007) that 'school' music provides little that challenges, has relevance or builds on what children already do. I think that in the early years if we only present children with music that is the equivalent of a limited diet of bland milky slops (five familiar nursery rhymes) then at home the analogous diet of burgers and chips will be much more appealing. But what I am proposing is a rich, satisfying and nutritious variety of musical experiences which is relevant to babies' and children's ages and stages of development, has the challenge that play offers, and builds on what they already know and do. This is what Froebel wanted for the children he taught 200 years ago and this is what we want for our children now.

Froebelian principles in this chapter

- Babies and young children need to sing and be sung to. Froebel realised the incredible opportunity young mothers were missing in the development of their children's capacities for learning. Much of his work was in developing songs, hand activities and games for mothers to play with their children.
- Connecting with home and community. Learning in school does not happen in isolation from the home. Froebel realised that the school and home should be united. Margaret McMillan was influenced by this view when she said that schools should reflect the finest of what a good family can offer: 'Best of homes, least of schools.'
- Play is the characteristic activity of young children and the way in which they learn best. Froebel realised, through observation, that play in childhood is the most effective way that children make sense of the world.
- Holistic learning. Froebel realised that there is a unity in children's learning. Children learn emotionally, socially, intellectually and physically all at the same time. Children learn the things that are connected with what they know already.
- Children learn through exploring opposites. Froebel realised that children discover connections with the opposite of its kind. Music gives lots of opportunities for exploring opposites.

Further reading

Books about offering musical experiences to young children

Evans, N. (2006) *Tuning into Children*. London: Youth Music.

Evans, N. (2008) *Reflections on Creative Music-making in the Early Years in Sound Progress*. London: Youth Music.

Goddard-Blythe, S. (2011) *The Genius of Natural Childhood*. Stroud: Hawthorn Press.

Pound, L. and Harrison, C. (2003) *Supporting Musical Development in the Early Years*. Buckingham: Open University Press.

Young, S. (2003) *Music with the Under Fours*. London: RoutledgeFalmer.

Young, S, and Glover, J. (1998) *Music in the Early Years*. Brighton: Falmer Press.

Local Authority guidance

Bretherick, H. (ed) (2004) *Sound Foundation – a Music Handbook for Early Years*. Rydeen: Croydon Early Years and Croydon Music Service.

Morrow, J. (2000) *Music – Early Years Activities to Promote Children's Creative Development*. Dunstable: Belair Publications.

Tower Hamlets (1997) *Making Music from Early Years to Key Stage 2*. London: Learning Design.

Song books sold with CDs

For a full list of A&C Black titles see: *www.acblack.com*

Geoghegan, L. (2002) *Singing and Rhymes for Early Years*. Glasgow: National Youth Choir of Scotland.

Matterson, E. (1969) *This Little Puffin*. London: Penguin Books.

McNicol, R. (2000) *Music Explorer for Infants*. London: London Symphony Orchestra Ltd.

Stories to use with instruments

Cooke, T. (1994) *So Much*. London: Walker Books.

And virtually any story book you use!!

CHAPTER 10

GIFTS AND OCCUPATIONS:

FROEBEL'S GIFTS (WOODEN BLOCK PLAY) AND OCCUPATIONS (CONSTRUCTION AND WORKSHOP EXPERIENCES) TODAY

JANE WHINNETT

Observations of children

Froebel encouraged his friends and followers to start by observing the child. This observation served two purposes – to know the child better in order to support their development and to gather information about how children learn. This chapter will focus on the use of some of the modern equivalents of the Froebelian Gifts (wooden blocks) and Occupations (construction and workshop experiences) and also follow the development of several children in the nursery school. Over a holiday, I had read some of Froebel's work in translation and reminded myself of the stages Harriet Johnson (1933) had developed to describe block play. She was a Froebel-trained teacher in the 1930s. This was further elaborated in the Froebel block-play research project (Gura, 1992). Children typically begin by stacking vertically or horizontally.

Figure 10.1 Alea's garage

Alea's garage shows horizontal stacking (Figure 10.1). Mathematically, it shows forms of knowledge in the one-to-one correspondence of the vehicles and equivalence in the matching up of the longer blocks with two shorter ones.

Keith's dragon shows vertical and horizontal stacking with effective use of the wedge to suggest scales (Figure 10.2).

Sinead's castle shows vertical stacking, bridging, vertical enclosures and symmetry (Figure 10.3). It exemplifies a form of beauty in its awareness of pattern. The blocks are carefully balanced both physically and visually. The arrangement of the blocks on the shelves encourages Sinead to select the ones she wants carefully and supports her ideas by having the same blocks stored in the same place. On the left-hand side of the cabinet, it is easy to see the relationship between the different sizes of block of unit, half, quarter and eighth.

Figure 10.2   Keith's dragon

Figure 10.3   Sinead's castle

Jacqueline explored the formula for multi-storey building by herself one day. She created a four-storey building fairly quickly. Then stood back to think about it. Gura (1992) describes children pausing to reflect on their learning in the blocks. Jacqueline is a reflective learner. Her building shows core and radial elaboration in the tower on top. She said it was a castle. Later she added a horizontal path with a spiral end to it. There is beauty in the creation of the symmetry. The building reflects her interest in fairytale, expressed in the core and radial schema.

When it was time to tidy up, Jacqueline realised how many blocks she had used and there was some regret at having to tidy them all up. The adult who had been observing, entering into her dominant play theme, commented that what was needed was a bit of magic! Jacqueline left and returned with a wand she had brought to nursery that day. She played along with the adult's theme by waving it and clearing the block's away herself. Another child arrived, observed, smiled and asked if he could have a shot. She handed him the wand and he entered the game, conspiring with the magic and helping to tidy voluntarily as a part of the shared game.

It is easy to observe a child in one area, but it is important to see the child as a whole, and Jacqueline, as well as enjoying wooden block play, engages with many occupations too. Her use of some of the Froebelian Occupations will be explored later in this chapter (see p. 131).

Co-operative block play

Aidan, William and Daniel. One of the great advantages of having younger and older children playing regularly together is the sharing of ideas and skills that takes place. Aidan is the eldest. Inspired by his aeroplane, made in the large hollow blocks using large blocks on end, to create height, with a plank between to sit on and another plank balanced on this to create wings, William, one of the younger children, attempts to make his own plane. On his first attempt, he manages to re-create the plank between the two blocks but finds that the wings will not balance. Gradually, he realises by pushing the plank to the centre that this is the balancing point. Older children show younger children what is possible. Froebel recognised how children learn with and through each other.

Later Daniel joins in. He sets a plank on a block, balancing it on the centre. He sits on the end and it swings to the floor. 'I've made a see-saw!' he announces.

A group of boys have been building with the unit blocks. There are three experienced builders and three younger children who are keen to join in. The older boys have a formula, called a module by Gura (1992: 80), to create a multi-storey building using rectangular boards and quarter unit blocks standing up on the smallest face. They build all around the bottom layer, taking turns to add bricks casually in the shared aim. Occasionally, they leave spaces or add a single or double eighth block. When the castle is finished, they have favourite characters to engage in a short, shared play theme. There seems to be little discussion or negotiation for figures with a general acceptance of who will have which figures – Nathan's dragon, Aidan's knight but they hold them in their hand as they build!

Block play learning from others' experimentation

One of the benefits of having older and younger children in the same group is the expertise that the older children bring to the experiences of the younger ones. By the summer term, some of our children are 5 years old and will have been in nursery for two years. Friendships develop across the age range by having something in common. Often block building brings children together. With support from an adult at times, children learn to respect others' ideas, in the concrete form of blocks, turn-taking and developing shared negotiated aims and spatial awareness as well as appreciation of others' work. Sometimes the adult takes a leading role in protecting one child's idea to allow this to develop for others to see. Children who are just becoming confident in any kind of expression need a sensitive audience who recognise their intentions and right to express themselves. For children with English as an additional language, this is equally important. Being fluent in one language but not understood by anyone is a potentially frightening or frustrating experience. Where possible, we place children with the same first language in the same group in nursery. We encourage use of first language so that children can continue to build concepts and socialise without the constant pressure of learning an additional language.

Children also learn from each other's ideas across the different sessions if they see photographs or the final model. The idea of building on a baseboard was introduced early by the adults as an option for stability and also as a visual reminder to define the builder's personal space when constructing. Sometimes children want to make their own buildings rather than contribute to a group project. It is important for children to see the cause and effect of their own actions on their building. Everyone goes through the learning process of the feelings of anger when someone else knocks down the building or adds blocks without negotiating to do so.

The multi-storey building, using baseboards, was originally developed in the afternoon session by a group of experienced blockies (Gura, 1992) with an adult. Children in the morning built enclosures, as outlines often one block high. They more often filled in enclosures. Later one child layered the enclosed area, using blocks and then covered them over with small boards.

In the afternoon, a younger child, who found sharing ideas and allowing others to build without his minor or major transformations a challenge, built on his own. He created a vast horizontal enclosure, finishing off with a vertical stack where he explored balance using a pattern of thick and thin cylinders. This was more characteristic of his building but he had seen other children creating enclosures in this way. Froebel maintained that in play children demonstrate their understanding at its highest level.

Observing children engaged in the Froebelian Occupations in the way that they are offered to children today

Froebel described his series of Gifts (wooden blocks) and Occupations as focusing on the progression of symbolic representation, beginning with the three-dimensional blocks, progressing to the faces of the blocks as two-dimensional shapes in the form of tiles, followed by lines (the edges of the shapes) in the form of sticks or thin spills of wood and, finally, to more plastic materials, for example, clay. (Froebel, in Brehony, 2001: 306–47).

Earlier in the chapter, Jacqueline's block play was described. Jacqueline's journey through different forms of symbolic representation has been fascinating to observe. She uses a wide range of symbolic representation to express her ideas successfully. The Froebelian Occupations pioneered this possibility, and continue to offer these opportunities today.

Jacqueline's drawing

At around the same time as her block play castle, Jacqueline drew a picture on a large piece of paper on the easel and wrote her name in capital letters. With ten letters to remember in her name, she often referred to her name label, but on this occasion she did not. A similar pattern of filled in enclosures can be seen in her drawing. Here too, she uses a formula she has developed. Athey (1990) described in some detail the relationships between children's schema and their graphic representations. There is a clear link between the trajectory schema in her building, the enclosures and trajectories in her name. The Es resemble the window construction formula. She forms letters in straight lines, adding a cross stroke to the J.

Jacqueline's graphic symbolic representation shows an abstract understanding of the significance of marks. She is bilingual and, as such, knows that forms can have more than one name. Research shows that many bilingual children come to understand symbolic representation sooner than monolingual children (Sorace, 2010). They come to realise that symbols represent, or stand for things, people and situations. Jacqueline was interested in Chinese script and explored creating the symbols for tiger as well as writing the word in English (Matthews, 2003: 145).

On this occasion, when her attention was focused on writing with a brush, she chose to glue her name on. Having pre-printed labels allows children to choose to write by themselves or communicate a message quickly while focusing on something else. Sometimes the shape or colour of the paper inspires a child to attempt graphic representation in the form of writing, for example, having folded card, stapled books or envelopes. A strip of paper about the size of their name label sometimes suggests writing to a child and they will do this spontaneously, revealing their competence.

As well as writing her name one day, Jacqueline also used visual graphic representation in an 'I love you' message. She used a heart shape for love and a y for you. Matthews (2003: 144) identifies these two different uses of images as symbols, which capture something of the shape of the represented object and signs, including letters, words and numbers. It was unusual for her to use y to represent you. She had often used this formula before, using a u; in the same way an adult uses it in text. The different use is interesting as it shows the beginning of a shift to knowledge of symbols to the alphabetic principle and more conventional use.

To help children find their own name, different coloured sticky spots are added to the top left corner of the name label. The position of the dot also emphasises visually the first letter of the name. On another occasion, Jacqueline had made a mark at the beginning of her name. When asked about the mark, she replied, 'it's the dot. It's oval because it's Easter!' Her remark shows another understanding of graphic representation and a sense of humour that she knows the adult will appreciate. Sharing humour with children allows the adult to enter into the world of their understanding, since for it to be a shared joke each must understand the other well and respectfully.

On her last few days in nursery, Jacqueline requested the princess dresses. She returned to the play theme that had been her abiding interest. She was absorbed all afternoon, changing costume, dancing and, finally, acting out the story of Snow White, with other children taking on roles. Late in the afternoon, staff asked her about having a snack. Children served themselves a snack when they wanted it. To help her make a decision about whether she wanted a snack or not, the adult informed in her a semi-serious tone that it was apple. She laughed knowingly and declined!

Practical work with children and families

The environment for learning plays an important role in a Froebelian approach to children's development. Froebel developed a progression of Gifts and Occupations to support children's development. The most famous of these are blocks, but these are only part of the system to support learning, particularly symbolic representation. Froebel placed great importance on the child's creativity, making the inner outer was a way of reaffirming humankind as a creative being and part of humanity. Anything the child makes or does can be seen as an expression of their understanding of the world around them. Their inner thoughts are demonstrated in the outer representations they make in whichever media they choose.

Initially, Froebel laid out very prescriptive ways in which his blocks were to be used. The series of Gifts structured the learning in ways that he thought would support children's development best. Later, he concluded that free play with the equipment revealed more about the child's development (Liebschner, 1992: 55).

Presentation of Gifts (wooden blocks)

The Gifts and Occupations came in a series of wooden boxes that were presented to the child in such a way that the Gift was uncovered whole. The child could then transform the Gift to learn about its properties, building a variety of models showing forms of life, knowledge and beauty. Examples of these can be seen in Liebschner (1992: 80). Froebel recognised the child's need to do things for himself to disassemble and reassemble forms. When the child was finished, the blocks were reassembled into a whole and returned to the box.

In the nursery, we have two different-sized sets of blocks and, although they are not kept in boxes, they are presented to children in the form of a whole. They are arranged on shelves sorted by shape. Each block has its place. Children are helped and encouraged to replace them when they are finished. Gradually, this becomes routine and part of the experience.

Children arrive in nursery with a wide range of knowledge and experiences. The mixed age groups allow children of 3 years to learn from and with their more experienced peers. The hollow blocks are often their first introduction to blocks, being unlike anything they are likely to have at home. They usually start by watching their peers, then try out ideas for themselves. Unit blocks are also attractive for knocking down, an activity that is not appreciated by the builders!

There are small world toys alongside the blocks. The proximity of their placement arose from children's interests or requests. Children used fairytale characters in the blocks for an extended period of time of several weeks. This arose from an interest in princesses and participation in the song 'There was a princess long ago' and in fairy stories in general. The nursery staff decided to extend children's interest beyond their understanding of the images presented to them in DVDs and commercial products. Many had princess dresses and wore them to occasions in the nursery. Some mentioned them when reviewing and planning their learning.

Small world characters from stories, legends, poems and rhymes

To give children a wider range of materials to develop their forms of representation, small world fairy story characters were displayed beside the unit blocks. This generated interest from a wide range of children – both boys and girls.

Some children initially represented the princess song in blocks as they had seen an adult do, singing to themselves and acting out the story with the figures. Other children became very interested in the structure of castles and used non-fiction books to refer to. This resulted in a range of buildings using enclosures.

Some children initially imitated the song using the characters to act it out. Other children began to make up their own stories using the characters and the blocks to build scenery for the action.

Drawing – the graphics table

During this time, the round graphics table was located nearby. The area had shelves with a variety of paper and writing implements available and area dividers that were used to display children's names on labels. These were fixed with Velcro for the children to detach if they wanted to refer to them. In addition there was a display of frequently requested words for writing cards, for example, to, love, from, mum, dad. Some children had a folder of their own words. A group of children drew and wrote regularly every day, building up a vocabulary of words by memory through constant use.

The small world characters were displayed with a photograph, a name label and their role. The children had a variety of ideas. Alternative labels were made later when the children wanted to take the cards to the graphics table to write their own stories. A character, identified as a queen by some children, was called a bad fairy by others. A knight to some children was a baddie to others and one figure was either a princess or a fairy. Some children played out their stories with the characters then came to write. 'Once upon a time' and 'They lived happily ever after' were added to the word board. Others went straight to writing, for them producing the words and having them read back was their aim.

Froebel described what he believed to be the most effective approach to the development of reading and writing in *Lina Learns to Read*. (Froebel, in Brehony 2001: 1–54). He describes the supportive relationship between Lina and her mother who supports her reading and writing by providing what she needs. The process starts with her name as a whole rather than individual letters, as this is the most important word to her. Her mother provides paper for writing letters to her father. Froebel commends her approach as a role model for others wishing to teach young children to read and write. Writing is a complex form of symbolic representation. Children need a wide range of experiences to draw on and lots of opportunities to represent their inner meanings in the outward representations in play.

Jacqueline represented her inner understandings of being a princess in many ways. She was supported in this in the nursery and also at home. Her parents added a page to her learning folio about how she had changed since she was a baby, with photographs and her scribed ideas. She said she liked to be on a swing as a baby and now she liked to dress up as a princess.

She became engrossed in fairy tales, often choosing to look at books by herself, recalling parts of the story and also interpreting the illustrations, sharing her ideas and inferences. She enjoyed dressing up to dance. Her dances became more co-operative with a partner and often travelling round and round. She learned to turn under her partner's arm. For those who are interested in schemas, this would suggest a core and radial schema.

In a more abstract representation, she used her own body as a core and a ribbon on a stick as Rapunzel's hair as a radial! Jacqueline's core and radial schema manifested itself in her other representations.

She used the unit blocks to create 'a glass roundabout'(Figure 10.4). She re-created this on another day with greater elaboration on the radials as 'garnishing' (Gura, 1992). In a group of children who meet and play together regularly, children learn from each other and can transform others' ideas for their own ends. Jacqueline used the multi-storey building of elaborate stacking enclosures, adding her own schema in a path with a core and radial spiral end using quarter circle blocks.

Construction kits – lines

Wei used a wide range of media to represent his ideas. His experiences reflect the progression in Froebel's series of Gifts and Occupations. Wei developed a sophisticated knowledge of shape, position, direction, planning – the elements of basic trigonometry! His abiding interest was vehicles, particularly planes. He created these in a wide range of models – from pieces of wood of different length and width; from construction kits which had strong linear components, for example, Lacy; and from construction kits based on the nets of three-dimensional shapes,for example, mobilo.

Paper-folding

Wei had a very good knowledge of shape. He used magnetic two-dimensional shapes to create a variety of representation – train tracks from rectangles, a car from circles, rectangles and triangles. He used his knowledge of shape and support from home to learn to fold paper aeroplanes. He became adept at creating the front point by folding each of the two corners in to meet exactly in the centre without having to create a central fold. The planes had a consistent, but complex design, to create a weighted front to help it to fly better. He was

Figure 10.4   Jaqueline's glass roundabout

generous in demonstrating and giving the planes away to others, always secure in the knowledge he could create more!

Paper-folding was a controversial topic in Froebelian circles of the past! Children choosing to transform paper into shapes that are meaningful to them is a valuable experience. Directing a large group of children step by step in an adult-directed activity is quite another! Elsie Murray (1903) challenged the emphasis on handwork in Froebelian practice in an article 'That symmetrical paper folding and symmetrical work with Gifts are a waste of time for both students and children' and created a storm of letters and complaints!

First-hand experiences

Froebel recognised the importance of the child's family and community to development. Children in the kindergarten were often seen in the town being involved in everyday life and seeing people at work. One of the annual events in the nursery calendar is the celebration of the poet Robert Burns's birthday, accompanied by an interest in Scottish culture. Visits to the Royal Mile in Edinburgh and the tartan museum often led to an interest in tartan patterns. This informs planning when resources are organised and presented to the children, particularly for creating with glue or sewing. Samples of tartan as reference are displayed so children can see the whole pattern. During this session, the gluing table was set out with rectangular baskets of strips of card of different colours in different widths and lengths, alongside wool of different colours. The children were free to choose what they wished to create, with a member of staff available to support if necessary and to talk through their ideas.

Weaving

Some children revisited the resources several times over several days. The adult demonstrated weaving and this was incorporated into different designs. Alea created a beautifully constructed mat. She had mastered weaving alternate warp threads with strips of card, creating a regular pattern. When she had completed the weaving, she went on to embellish the edges of the mat by cutting squares that exactly matched the size of the space between the woven pattern and the edge of the mat. This matching up is very like her positioning of the vehicles, one on each block, in the first example in this chapter. This interest was also transferred outside to weave with recycled plastic bags on the fence.

Even, an older child, investigated a range of ideas using the strips to fold in a concertina, make loops, weave and transform the long strips into pieces. She created a series of collages using a variety of techniques. In her first attempt, she created a cross over horizontal strips on a plain rectangle of paper. She went on to use a piece of paper pre-cut for weaving to create a loop. Later, she created a selection of techniques on the same baseboard – weaving, concertina folding and loops. A younger child joined her in play, beginning to use her resources. She allowed him to add to her creation – sharing an indulgent smile with the watching adult. She was used to working with and making allowances for her younger brother. This work became a process of adding different shapes cut from the strips and lengths of wool, placed in circular movements. The act of the creation became the creation itself. The final collaboration was an equal partnership.

Plastic or malleable materials and lines

One day Jacqueline and Wei sat next to each other at the clay. Wei began to roll long thin sausages of clay. He used the clay lines to write words. By this point in the year, he could write all of his family's names in full. The repeated W in his names caused him no trouble at all from when he was 3 years old.

Originally, he wrote his name in capital letters then moved on to well-formed capital and lower case letters. He could write several words quickly, accurately and independently. POLICE was one of his favourites. He developed long story lines in a comic style format from top to bottom of his page and from left to right. Wei learned to read his name early in his nursery career and could read all of the children's names in his class. When interpreting a recipe to bake, he correctly identified Wei in the word 'weigh' in the instructions and laughed at the pun!

Jacqueline used the clay lines in a different way to represent her family. She used the thin clay sausages like lines to draw them (Figure 10.5). Froebel gave a great deal of detail about how drawing could be sequenced for children. Nowadays this would seem very formal and adult directed. It encouraged a very prescriptive approach like technical drawing, based on grids and joining points. However Wei's spontaneous drawing on one occasion exemplifies this. He had helped to put up the class artificial Christmas tree. The tree had lights and was waiting for children to make decorations. Wei thought the tree should have a star on top. He chose gold card. Expertly, he drew freehand a five-pointed star using a formula of five straight lines on the reverse side, which was white. He knew exactly how long each line should be and joined the final line to meet the starting point. He cut it out but wanted both sides of the star to be gold, so

Figure 10.5   Representations in clay lines

used his star as a template to make another. Another child used a different technique, creating a star by cutting his own triangles and sticking these around a central shape.

Children need opportunities to show what they know through open-ended experiences and equipment. These opportunities can be built on the Froebelian Gifts and Occupations. Wei would not have been able to demonstrate his skills in geometry without a real problem to solve to demonstrate them. The adults that work with young children have to be well educated themselves to see the potential for learning in children's representations, to be able to identify the learning and see the possible next steps in the broadest terms but leading on to subject specific knowledge. One of the benefits of the Scottish *Curriculum for Excellence* (Scottish Executive, Learning and Teaching Scotland, 2009) is that it is intended for children from the age of 3 until 18. Both experiences and outcomes are important. A child's possible learning could be charted through the strands with outcomes at different levels. It is possible to see where a child demonstrating his knowledge of shape, position and movement at the early level may reach by the third level. The progression is laid out for all staff to see at whatever level they are working at with that child.

Froebelian principles in this chapter

- Recognition of the uniqueness of each child's capacity and potential. Observing each child reveals their individual interests and a depth of information about their development. Knowing each child well helps adults to plan for their development in a way that is going to extend it. Starting where the child is rather than from preconceived activities makes learning personal, relevant and coherent. Knowledge of child development and how children learn helps everyone working with the child provide for each child.
- A holistic view of each child's development. Observation of children in spontaneous play reveals their understanding. Young children do not conceptualise their learning in subject areas. Spontaneous self-chosen activity or play reveals what they know and their interests. Analysis of observations can reveal their learning in different areas of a curriculum. The whole of children's learning can be much more than the sum of its parts. The whole can transform what has been learned before into new understandings – a bit like a chemical reaction can transform two different substances into one new one. An example of this is Wei's developing understanding of literacy. He knows his name as a whole and also as a sequence of particular parts, letters. He notices the sequence of letters in the word 'weigh' but laughs because he understands that this is a word that has more than one meaning and that this can create a language game that is funny, making a pun.

- Recognition of the importance of play as a central integrating element in a child's development and learning. Jacqueline's play reveals her interest in enclosing, core and radial schema. These schema permeate her interactions with the environment. Her enduring interest manifests itself in the princess theme in her play. She dresses up in long dresses enclosing herself, she dances with a partner round and round, she uses a long ribbon as Rapunzel's hair, she builds towers and acts out 'Princess long ago', she builds a multi-storey castle of enclosed floors and adds a core and radial path, she uses clay to create figures of enclosed lines and sculptures using sticks garnished with balls of clay. Her graphic representations reflect her growing under-standing of communication through writing and drawing. Evidence of her schema are present here too. The rich range of resources provided allow Jacqueline to explore and represent her ideas in many ways – to make the outer inner and the inner outer.
- Recognition of the child as part of a family and community. Parents make a unique contribution to their child's learning. Each child's identity is formed in relation to self, family and community. Everyone working with young children has to learn as much as possible from parents to understand the child. Learning about the physical, cultural, linguistic and social community the child lives in will give us all a better-informed picture of the child. As well as observations and information from parents, nursery staff need time to reflect and learn themselves with opportunities for continued profes-sional development at their level. They have to be well-informed about influences on children, understand how different circumstances affect them and how they can support each child and family better.

Reflective questions and practical actions

- How do you provide for individual children's development in symbolic repre-sentation in the resources that you provide?
- Observe how an individual child is using your provision over several sessions. Reflect on the child's use of resources and your role in developing the child's learning further.

Introductory reading

Bruce, T. (2011a) *Early Childhood Education*. 4th edn. London: Hodder Arnold.

Gura, P. (ed.) (1992) *Exploring Learning: Young Children and Blockplay*. London: Paul Chapman Publishing.

Liebschner, J. (1992) *A Child's Work: Freedom and Guidance in Froebel's Theory and Practice*. Cambridge: Lutterworth Press.

Further reading 📖

Athey, C. (1990) *Extending Thought in Young Children: A Parent–Teacher Partnership*. London: Paul Chapman Publishing.

Brehony, K.J. (2000) 'English revisionist Froebelians and schooling of the urban poor', in M. Hilton and P. Hirsch (eds), *Practical Visionaries: Women, Education and Social Progress 1790–1930*. Harlow: Pearson Education.

Brehony, K.J. (2001) *The Origins of Nursery Education: Friedrich Froebel and The English System, Vol 4 Friedrich Froebel's Education by Development*. Trans. Josephine Jarvis. London and New York: Routledge.

Murray, E.R. (1903) 'That symmetrical paper folding and symmetrical work with Gifts are a waste of time for both students and children', *Child Life*, 17: 14–18.

CHAPTER 11

FROEBELIAN METHODS IN THE MODERN WORLD: A CASE OF COOKING

CHRIS McCORMICK

Fatimah – observations of a child learning through cooking opportunities. Reflections of a Froebelian experience.

Background

Fatimah comes from an extended and very close Pakistani family. The Asian culture of cooking is very important at home and observation of and involvement in cooking and food preparation is significant in the lives of the children. Fatimah came to nursery aged 3 – alongside her sister who had already been in the nursery for a year. She knew little English at this point.

Starting at nursery

Fatimah presented as a shy, sensitive and anxious child who had not previously experienced separation from Mum and Dad. She experienced a prolonged and upsetting settling-in process. First each weekend and then each school holiday break was followed by further upset for Fatimah and, following an extended family trip to Pakistan there was a clear need to start the settling process again. Close working between home and nursery enabled her to be supported through short periods of attendance with one parent or her aunt present. She progressed to managing short periods in the nursery with her sister for support. She stayed close to her sister then progressed to staying close to a nursery adult. During this time she was often tearful and unable to engage in many learning experiences. She then progressed to spending short periods observing from her chosen 'safe spot'. Although she spoke to her sister, no verbal communication was attempted with adults.

Engagement begins

Fatimah's chosen spot was close to the snack/baking table and it appeared that she was interested in observing food preparation activities. This gave us our first clue towards supporting and engaging with her. She began to come closer to and then to sit at the table. She began to respond to an adult's comment with eye contact and later a nod or shake of her head. She began to initiate communication by pointing. One day she accepted the offer of taking part and so began her engagement in nursery cooking experiences.

Widening of experiences

It quickly became evident that Fatimah was skilled in a variety of food preparation related tasks. She ably handled all processes and became confident to reveal this. She became able to work co-operatively and to share her skills with others. Gradually language related to these activities was developed. She then began to transfer her interest in food to other areas of learning.

Recorded observations of Fatimah

This is the story of Fatimah's learning journey told through recorded observations made of her in the nursery. These are presented in chronological order over a two-year period.

Figure 11.1   Involvement begins – Fatimah matching vegetables with illustrations in the cookbook

- Fatimah indicated that she wanted to stir the cake mixture. She did this very ably and seriously. Handed the bowl back to me when she was finished. Made eye contact for affirmation.
- Observing and handling vegetables for soup making. Silently matched each one to photos in cookbook. Looked for affirmation (Figure 11.1).
- Very focused on her task of weighing ingredients for her recipe. Watched the scales carefully. Patiently made fine adjustments (a little more flour, a little less sugar) to achieve an exact result.
- Observed apples before we cut them up for a snack. Made an excellent drawing of an apple. Large scale, included detail of stalk. Subtly shaded the 'skin' to achieve realistic effect.
- Used collage materials to create a picture of an apple tree.
- Independently followed pictorial recipe for making pancake batter (Figure 11.2). Organised, measured and mixed ingredients effectively and confidently. Observed the cooking of the pancakes on the griddle. Used a long-handled lifter to turn the pancakes over and to remove them to a plate. Washed up her dishes then went to the drawing table and drew 'Fatimah's pancake'.
- Pointed to cereal indicating that she was hungry. 'I want.' Helped herself taking account of a sign telling her how many spoonfuls. Observed the writing on the milk jug (milk, cream). Dealt with her dishes when finished and wiped the table.

Figure 11.2   True skills revealed – Fatimah independently preparing her pancake batter

- Fatimah capably cut up a banana into evenly sized pieces.
- Interested in the use of electricity (plug, wire, switch, light) for mixer.
- Enjoyed using smoothie maker. Carefully added honey and yoghurt to fruits she had helped to prepare. A little nervous of the noise at first, but as she had control of the 'pulsing' she experimented with short and longer bursts. Interested in the change in the mixture.
- Following washing dishes Fatimah laid out all the plates in a row and counted them. 'For giving to peoples. One, two, three …'
- Indicated her desire to dry dishes that another child was washing by pointing to the dish towel. 'I do that.'
- Role play around 'Handa's Surprise' story. Fatimah carried a basket with food items in it on her head.
- Chose a friend to help her bake her birthday cake. Managed to cope with the celebration although shy of the attention. Wore the birthday hat!
- Concentrated well on her baking activity. Didn't ask for Dad or need to see him at all this morning.
- Enjoyed using the food processor to grate carrots.
- Smelling freshly grated carrots and saying, 'yum.'
- Using hand grater to grate cheese for muffins. 'Yum.'
- Playing in house corner – food preparation activities. Setting table, matching dishes and sharing out play dough food.
- Comparing soy sauce to 'Pepsi' by its appearance.

- Spent an extended period of time mixing cornflour and water to make 'gluck'. Fascinated by the resulting texture, explored its qualities repeatedly.
- Enjoyed pancake poem and illustrated it with a drawing of herself tossing a pancake.
- Decorating shortbread mixture by pricking it with a fork. 'I was digging with the fork.'
- Drew individual fruits for snack menu.
- Cutting up play dough to make tiny cakes for a new cake stand in the house corner. Displayed these and carried them around the nursery offering them to adults and children in the room.
- Observed variety of flavours in ice-cream shop. Chose strawberry. Enjoyed eating this.
- Ice cream shop role play. Fatimah dressed in the hat and jacket. Selling ice-cream cones to her friends. 'What kind you want?' recalling flavours we had seen in the shop 'vanilla, strawberry, blue?'
- Helping to wash and cut up plums we were given by a parent to taste and to make jam with. Later represented plums with play dough – very realistic in size, shape and detail.
- Observing photographs of the visit of the hens to the nursery. Fatimah used watercolours to create a detailed painting of a hen. Carefully created the speckled effect of the feathers. Worked on it until she was happy with her result.
- Experimented with chopsticks. Persevered to use them in one hand.
- Prepared, cooked and presented egg pancake and rice rolls for her classmates. Demonstrated advanced skills – helped others to do this.
- Making play dough cakes. Carefully placed sparkly 'snowflakes' on top of each one to decorate them.
- Followed pictorial recipe book to make two sponge cakes, one for herself and one to give to a friend. Later helping others to follow the same process.
- Decorated gingerbread man biscuit. Carefully piped a line around the outside edge, created facial features and buttons. Added zigzag patterns. Later drew similar patterns onto a paper gingerbread man.
- Looking at 'Gingerbread Man' story – Fatimah compared the illustration of GM to her decorated biscuit.
- Role-playing birthday celebration with I. Cut straws into tiny pieces to decorate around the cake and then used larger pieces to make the candles. 'Four – like Fatimah's birthday cake!'
- Involved with interest and excitement in planting of an apple tree. Looking at life-cycle book to follow seasonal processes. Recalled that the tree was bought with money made from selling plum jam she helped to make.
- Making roti with play dough. Slapping dough from hand to hand. 'Like mummy does.' Shared roti with others taking it around the nursery on a tray she had set. Tearing them into small pieces.

- Followed all processes to make a Halloween Jack O'Lantern. Helped to scoop out pumpkin pulp and separated seeds from flesh. Drew face on it. Delighted when candle was lit and she joined in the Jack O'Lantern song.
- Ducking for apples with a fork. Observed that the apples floated and laughed as they bobbed about.
- Made a collage picture of an apple tree and recalled her tree planting experience. 'We made a big hole. I digged it. We put the baby tree in. That was two baby trees. I was getting water for it 'cos it needs a drink. Apples will be on it in a long time – like this (pointing to apples in her picture).'
- Independently baked sponge cake for her birthday celebration. Anticipating the party with excitement. 'It's my birthday and I'm five now! I baked my cake and Anya helped me – she's my friend. I put in five candles. You sing Happy Birthday to me … and a card with five on it!'
- Made a drawing of herself at nursery which reflected her favourite experiences. The baking pinny was a significant symbol.

Reflecting on learning

Fatimah's personal learning folder was very important to her. She enjoyed looking at the photographs and as her skills in English developed her responses and comments were recorded and she enjoyed looking at her personal learning planning folder and made lots of reflective comments. She is very interested in the fact that comment slips beside the photographs of her early experiences were blank, remembering with a smile that it took her a while to start talking to us. Fatimah confidently made reflective comments on these early experiences and is very aware of her progress.

Answering questions about her nursery experiences:

What do you do here? 'Baking … that's my favourite!'
What do you like doing best? 'Baking … cakes, pancakes, bread and biscuits … and jam.'

She showed pride in her skills and awareness of her progress. She became able to plan for her chosen working activities, to assemble utensils and ingredients and to reflect on her experiences. Evidence was there that all curricular areas were being developed through her passion for cooking.

The drawing

Fatimah's final reflection on her nursery experience as she was preparing for primary school was a drawing (Figure 11.3):

Figure 11.3   Fatimah's drawing

This is me at my nursery. I am always happy. This is the love (heart area). This is the fashion (earrings). Do you know what this is? It's my pinny … for baking. I like baking. I can do it with you and I can do it all by myself. This is the plants that I was growing – potatoes. I gave them some water and I picked them in the bucket. This is my name and this is the frame – it's a decoration for my picture.

Froebelian foundations

It is apparent from the story told by these observations that Fatimah's innate love of cooking led her into developing her learning across all areas of the curriculum. The ethos of the nursery is based soundly on Froebelian principles and practice. This is the foundation that underpinned the experiences that made up Fatimah's journey and ensured successful outcomes for her, and is explained in more detail in the section entitled 'Froebelian principles in this chapter'.

Looking at cooking

Links between Froebelian thinking and opportunities related to cooking can be explored through consideration of some of the materials, processes and principles involved.

Exploration, use and research of a wide range of food and items and ingredients help children to engage with the familiar and to move forward into new and unfamiliar territory. This also demonstrates and teaches value and respect for each child and his or her family.

Learning about tools and utensils, from the simple use of hands for mixing, through experiencing a variety of kitchen equipment to the use of technological electrical equipment, means engagement in skills for life, real tasks in real contexts, adults and children working together and linking of learning across the curriculum.

Processes involved include use of recipes and making our own; shopping (what do we need? lists and recipes) and creating our own results. These experiences promote working together, developing independence and venturing into the wider environment.

Experiences relating to preparing and organising for cooking give an early experience of skills for learning throughout life. Children have the opportunity to explore these further in freeflow play.

Sharing of baking processes of preparing, mixing and measuring help children to develop confidence and independence and involve learning through the senses. Later experiences of independent baking help children to build on early experiences to apply their knowledge and understanding and to problem solve within the context of a real and meaningful task.

Most of the principles arising from cooking opportunities promote learning right across the curriculum and demonstrate Froebel's values of valuing childhood as a stage in itself, the importance of a holistic approach to children's learning, using the senses, learning and valuing nature. Promotion of the importance of healthy eating leads us into considering nutritional values, looking at snacks and lunches and helping children to be aware of appropriate balance.

Sharing of cultural celebrations encourages mutual respect, understanding and caring and helps children move through awareness of self, of others and of the wider world.

Cooking leads us naturally into consideration of eco-issues: growing foods, sourcing foods (food miles) recycling and composting. This brings children an understanding of nature's patterns and an awareness of the need to value and protect these.

Other world issues that link to this subject include equality and fairness, poverty and hunger. Children learn about circumstances in other countries and develop awareness of the importance of using what food we have and not wasting food (what can we make with these leftovers?). We explore Fairtrade issues in ways which help children to develop ethical values.

Practical issues for consideration include health and safety and food hygiene. Time and careful thought have to go into planning and providing spaces for cooking. This will very much depend on individual settings.

Health and safety matters are of vital importance and should support planned activities rather than limit them. With appropriate planning and assessments in place we can proceed with confidence. Children need to learn about the importance of hygiene and safety matters. Through experience and involvement they can learn about assessment of risk, a valuable skill for life.

Cooking is one of Froebel's Occupations which relates to real life, involves the child in real and practical work, encourages motivation, develops independence and promotes cross-curricular learning.

Circumstances alter cases

Those with a particular passion for any aspect of learning and teaching will always find ways of incorporating this into their practice. As a keen believer in the value and importance of cooking with young children, I have had to contend with the challenges posed by practising cooking in a variety of early years settings.

Modern purpose-built nursery school

This centre was jointly run by education and health services and was situated in an area of multiple deprivation on the edge of a small Scottish town.

In one corner of a large open-plan space a kitchen and snack area was provided. The area was confined, dark with little natural light and not easily visible from around the play area. The surrounding areas were all carpeted.

Staff presented the area as attractively as possible with small café-style tables and chairs, cheerful tablecloths and, usually, a cooking-related display. The presence of an adult made the area more inviting. There was a focus on snack preparation, and baking was provided as an occasional activity. Although sometimes limited in their experiences, the children were very enthusiastic about life, and play was the perfect medium through which to promote their learning. Language development was of key importance.

Cooking activities were built around the use of all the senses. Observation, discussion and hands-on experience captured their interest. Skills developed and many interesting responses were noted. Several terms developed by children were adopted and stay with me still; for example, flapjacks referred to as 'snackjacks', and the pumpkin that became known as a 'plumpkin'. Children come up with the best words!

Nursery class in a primary school

The nursery class was accommodated in an outbuilding within the playground of a small primary school in a run-down area where families coped with poor living conditions and a major drug culture. A large double classroom with a smaller single room at each end comprised the indoor provision, and an area of concrete playground was fenced off to provide an area for outdoor play.

Cooking was accommodated within the main playroom where all children could easily access the opportunities. A small kitchen area was provided with a baking table in the centre. Next to this we set up a large snack table with chairs. Ingredients were stored in the area. The table was usually decorated with flowers and an adult was always present to attract the children's interest and presence.

Children enjoyed food and were keen to eat, but were often limited in taste experiences and in shared experience around the table. The main focus was to present, observe and use a variety of ingredients with the children and to introduce new tastes. The niceties of sitting at table were developed and many comments and conversations were exchanged; for example a child made a loud exclamation shortly after sitting down at the snack table. When I turned to see what had happened she was staring ahead at the table and, after a moment, said, 'What a beautiful flooer!' – a rosebud which had opened up in the warmth of the room into a full blown flower head. She was right. It was beautiful!

American classroom

During an American exchange teaching opportunity I found myself in a hot, humid and dusty kindergarten classroom in an elementary school in Miami, Florida. This was an area of mixed races and cultures where many families struggled with poverty. Resources were limited and the classroom consisted of tables and chairs. Cooking did not feature on the curriculum.

As I developed my understanding of American culture and shared aspects of Scottish culture, the classroom took on a more cheerful aspect with a growing display of related materials carefully selected and carried from home. Of course, food and cooking had to feature – to the amazement of the other teachers who could not imagine how I was going to do this, or why!

I experienced my first (and only!) Hallowe'en celebration, in the baking heat with pumpkins galore. We looked at pancakes as enjoyed by each culture and made both varieties, cooked on an electric frying pan. How small traditional Scottish pancakes looked! We also explored soup-making, with preparation being done in the classroom and the soup cooked in the teachers' lounge. We shared the joy of crumbly shortbread – so easy to make and so delicious. I was asked to make this so many times during my year's visit, for every social occasion, and the children shared the recipe and experience at home.

Teachers from other grades marched their classes regularly through my classroom to see what the Scottish teacher was up to, and parents were invited to share our experiences. This exchange of cultural interests was rich and formed the focus of happy times, and the building of rewarding relationships.

Primary one classroom

This experience took place within a large traditional city primary school in an affluent area. The medium-sized classroom was packed full of tables and chairs. Access was available to a shared cooking space but this was not nearby and was difficult to organise with a full class. I chose to develop a shared cooking experience at Christmas, with a plan which I developed with children and parents to make a Christmas cake: language and mathematics around the recipe and the weighing of ingredients; social studies around the sources of ingredients; and art and craft to make cards recording children's ideas.

This took on a uniting focus. An inspired parent wrote a delightful poem about the baking of the 'Primary One Christmas Cake' – the ingredients, the sights, smells and tastes, the processes and the sharing of a magical experience. We used this as a focus for the preparation and baking. Everyone stirred the mixture and made a wish. The delicious smells of the cooking were enjoyed. We wrote our own poetry as we reflected on the experiences of baking, and tasting the cake. Truly cross-curricular learning!

Under-5s centre

This centre was a community resource for under-5s and their families, based within a high school. The centre was a very exciting and innovative place to be. Parents and their children of all ages, but mainly under 3, attended together on a drop-in basis, and stayed for their own chosen length of time. The focus here was on relationships – adults and children playing and learning together. Parents, many of whom had limited support networks, got to know each other and shared a whole variety of experiences on which to build closeness. What better uniting opportunity than cooking!

We were based initially in a small classroom and later, as numbers steadily increased, we were re-housed in a large and airy classroom that had been a cookery room. We created an attractive cooking area with pride of place given to a child-sized pine dresser, complete in every detail, made and gifted to us by a high school pupil. This was used for storage and display purposes, and it regularly reflected the seasons and interests we shared.

Baking was tricky with 2-year-olds – especially as everyone was keen for their child to take part. We progressed this by developing bread-making in the nursery. Staff started their day early by making two batches of dough. What a delightful start to the working day – planning the day as we kneaded the dough. One batch was cooked so as to be ready for snacks, while the other was left rising until folk arrived. This magic bread dough could be shared widely to accommodate all – adults helped children to knead, roll and shape the dough. Latecomers came straight to the table to join in and dough was further shared. We sang songs as we worked.

Gradually we extended this activity for the children – tiny individual loaf tins had to be greased and the dough squeezed in. Pastry brushes were used to coat the surface with milk. Seeds were scattered on top. The cooked loaves were ready by now and shared with everyone – sometimes plain slices, sometimes with butter, jam, lemon curd or cheese.

Parents used the recipe at home. Following a weekend break, a parent told us of suddenly remembering during a carpet-laying activity with her sister, that she had no bread for the children's tea … 'It was great I didn't even have to go out because I just went and made some!' … much to her sister's surprise. What a wonderful, significant, practical and uniting activity cooking proves to be.

Traditional nursery school

This is an idyllic setting – a small nursery school surrounded by a beautiful garden. Tall windows all round ensure plenty of light and a view dominated by the seasons. Children experience free flow of play between classroom and garden.

The nursery has a unique and historic feature of a series of stained-glass panels which represent a day in the life of children at play. Made especially for the school by artist William Wilson in 1934, the windows are a rare example of secular stained glass. The panels represent storytelling, gardening, circle games, see-saw, skipping, scooters, fishing, feeding birds, tending flowers, sleeping and, of course, eating.

The children come from a wide surrounding area and represent a mixture of race and culture. Bathed in the light of the windows, children and adults engage in food preparation activities daily. The nursery kitchen area is right in the centre of the room, 'the heart of the home', and provides maximum opportunity for children to participate and to observe both in a focused way, and just in passing. Development of the *Curriculum for Excellence* (Scottish Executive, Learning and Teaching Scotland, 2009) has helped us to know and understand that cooking is a key activity for learning. Experiences cut across and firmly link all areas of learning.

Activities carried out in this area are central to the work of the room. A galley kitchen arrangement is provided with a long, low worktop between the cooker area and the food preparation area. The worktop provides space for display, as well as for hand-washing. A large table is used for food preparation, baking and snack purposes and allows for room to work as well as to 'cluster round', for example, when observing the magic moments of the balancing of the scales.

Activities are very varied. Some are routine, for example, play dough making or fruit preparation. Some are child led, for example, ice cream interest or gingerbread men. Some are linked to the seasons, for example, cooking with apples or Christmas cake. Some are responsive to events, for example, a gift of plums led to crumble-making and jam. Some are linked to cultural celebrations, for example, 'surprise' birthday cakes, Asian cooking carried out by parents, or linked to festivals. Some relate to wider global issues, for example, Fairtrade.

Cooking contributes in so many ways to the ethos of our school. It is a caring and sharing activity. Sensitive adults and children work and learn together. Trust is built between participants. Each child can have the balance of support and independence that best suits their needs.

Global citizenship issues are naturally raised and addressed, for example, Fairtrade and environmental issues, leading to the award of a green eco-flag.

Parents become involved and enjoy sharing their culture, their love of cooking and their traditional ingredients and dishes. This builds positive links between home and school.

Health promotion is embedded in the practice of cooking – hand-washing, general hygiene, food handling and storage, healthy foods and an awareness of a balanced approach to eating.

Growing of the vegetables leads us into plant life cycles and seasonal activity in the garden. It raises issues of poverty and hunger, and leads us into supporting Comic Relief and Children in Need.

Through these activities, learning flows and links in a natural, meaningful and powerful way across all aspects of the curriculum. Whatever the circumstances of the setting, it is possible to effectively provide creative cooking opportunities – and how worthwhile!

Cooking up the curriculum

Carved around the head of the ceremonial mace which sits in the Scottish Parliament chamber are four words which reflect the cultural values of the Scottish people: *wisdom*, *justice*, *compassion* and *integrity*.

The Scottish *Curriculum for Excellence 3–18* (Scottish Executive, Learning and Teaching Scotland, 2009) gives us clear guidelines for supporting children's learning. At an aspirational level the four purposes of the curriculum reflect these values. We aim to support our learners to become successful learners, confident individuals, responsible citizens and effective contributors.

The principal vehicles for achieving this marry perfectly with Froebelian principles of practice. The importance of play is highlighted. Children are actively engaged in their own learning. Using observation-based assessment methods, teachers work with learners to recognise skill levels and to plan for the next steps in learning. Awareness of the child's skills, abilities and interests enables us to build on their intrinsic motivation to achieve the best possible results.

Eight curricular areas with suggested learning opportunities are defined to embrace the content of learning. Cross-cutting priorities of health and well-being, literacy and numeracy are recognised as essential components of all learning experiences and are embedded in the wider curriculum experience. Learning involves matching links and this cross-curricular approach ensures maximum opportunity for learning.

Seven guiding principles for curriculum design underpin delivery:

- challenge and enjoyment
- personalisation and choice
- progression
- depth
- coherence
- breadth
- balance.

The combination of these is powerful.

With a starting point of getting to know the child and the family we observe, support and extend learning; giving consideration to the key elements of the process of learning, the content of learning and the context within which learning takes place.

Cooking and the curriculum: some related experiences

Health and well-being has themes of emotional, personal and social development; physical development; food and health; planning for choices and changes. Related cooking experiences include:

- Fatimah's story – confidence and well-being, links between home and nursery, cultural links
- children using senses to explore and investigate a variety of foods and ingredients
- satisfaction of working independently, for example, cereal bar for children's use, juice squeezing to make drinks, making sponge cakes
- children 'A' and 'J' building a relationship. Sharing experience of looking through a cookbook together, studying recipes, commenting on content, sharing thoughts and ideas, laughing
- child 'I' helping another child with a broken arm to complete an independent baking activity by holding his baking bowl steady.

Literacy has themes of talking, listening, reading and writing. Related cooking experiences include:

- child 'L', with no English as yet, settling in nursery, competently followed a pictorial recipe to participate in what was obviously a familiar experience for her
- recording of cooking experiences either pictorially or copying writing

- children listening to instructions, explaining instructions to others
- responding to stimulus of activity at baking/snack table by sharing home experiences of food and cooking.

Numeracy has themes of number, measure, shape, position, movement, patterns, time and information-handling. Related cooking experiences include:

- skilled use of balance scales for weighing of ingredients. Children able to make precision adjustments and to use related mathematical language
- use of clock and of timers (sand and digital) to measure cooking times
- shopping experiences (real, role play and board games!) to explore ingredients, money and shops
- use of charts to record children's responses to foods/favourite snacks and so on.

Science has themes of senses, biology, the wonder of nature, forces and electricity, planet Earth and problem-solving. Related cooking experiences include:

- mixing of ingredients, change of state, application of heat and cold
- growing vegetables in the nursery garden
- use of electricity
- egg experiments involving a group of children in examining the properties of eggs
- child 'E' whose egg cracked but missed the bowl and landed on the floor. We laughed about this and he described it as 'the flying egg'. He went on to apply this description in similar situations where he observed falling items.

Technology has themes of recycling, information and communication technology (ICT), food technology, craft and design technology. Related cooking experiences include:

- recycling experiences and opportunities
- use of utensils and electrical equipment
- recognising that technology can help us, for example, beating egg whites with hand-whisk then using electric mixer
- problem-solving.

Social studies has themes of people who help us, our environment, the wider world and links with the past. Related cooking experiences include:

- visits by groups of children to Gladstone's Land (National Trust) to see how people lived long ago. Observation of kitchen, how it looked and what was there (and importantly, not there!)
- use of a wide range of cookbooks linking to awareness of professional cooks, for example, Delia Smith and Jamie Oliver who children may see on television

- • exploring of themes, for example, Fairtrade, Comic Relief, to look at circumstances of others in the world and to raise awareness of global issues.

Religious and moral education has themes of caring, sharing and co-operating, respect and understanding, the importance of celebrations and exploring beliefs. Related cooking experiences include:

- celebrating birthdays of children and staff. The fun of keeping the secret and then sharing the celebration, experiencing the warmth and the happiness of this
- child 'O' (Scottish) who so much enjoyed eating Chinese food with chopsticks that he kept a photograph of this on his bedroom wall. 'I really *love* Chinese New Year' he told us often!
- sharing of cultural celebrations leading to understanding of beliefs and values.

Expressive Arts has themes of art and craft, drama and role play, music and performance. Related cooking experiences include:

- exploring and recording form, for example, spontaneous painting of ingredients, use of art and craft materials, and techniques in response to 'still life' observation
- use of 'working' songs and rhymes to support and extend engagement, for example, when making bread. Children 'G' and 'F' very excited in play. They enjoyed exploring flour remnants on baking table and we provided a tray, dishes, spoons and flour as an activity for them. When they became overexcited in play this was a calming activity for them. The use of a song which included their names helped to extend their interest. 'G' would say 'Sing, sing!' They were very happy when their song was included in singing sessions and would ask for it.

Froebelian theory promotes play as an integrating mechanism which enables children to link and organise learning, and to reach the deepest levels of learning.

The *Curriculum for Excellence* underpinned by, and intertwined with, Froebelian theory and practice provides the strongest foundation on which we can build to enable children to achieve their full potential. This is surely the route towards the aspirational heights of the Scottish curriculum towards becoming successful learners, confident individuals, effective contributors and responsible citizens.

Conclusion

Froebel's educational vision and theories have continued to influence early years practice across the western world.

Froebelian practitioners develop a sound philosophy of practice based on their professional knowledge, understanding and experience. This underpins their approach to learning and teaching. They build on this by taking account of new developments in research and practice to ensure continuing relevance and the best possible standards of practice.

Froebel's themes of respect for the child, holistic education, harmony between subjects, the importance of play, real tasks in real contexts and the importance of children and adults working and learning together lend themselves perfectly to promotion of the principles, practice and delivery of the Scottish *Curriculum for Excellence*.

Children who are rocked in the Froebelian cradle grow and learn in the very best possible circumstances and gain an all important view of the world as a whole. 'Link only link.'

As a universal feature of daily living, 'food preparation' crosses all cultures and carries the potential for uniting families, friends, strangers and cultures in promotion of shared learning at the deepest level. Such activities are significant in the lives of children. Cooking provides real and meaningful contexts which capture their interest. This promotes the intrinsic motivation that leads to effective learning.

Many aspects of Froebelian theory can be closely linked with the practice of cooking giving it an important role to play in supporting learning and teaching. Recognition of this based on strong pedagogical principles and extensive classroom practice gives me passion to put forward … the case for cooking.

Froebelian principles in this chapter

Key Froebelian principles referenced in this chapter:

- Childhood as a valid stage of development within its own right
- Consideration of the child's holistic development
- Importance of family – feeling loved and valued
- Play as an integrating mechanism, helping children to bring together and organise learning
- Play helps children to reach the deepest levels of learning
- Value of self-activity within a framework of guidance
- Importance of learning through the senses
- Importance of real experiences in real contexts
- Importance of making links across learning to develop awareness of the unity of life
- Importance of nature – with harmony and natural connections
- Importance of adults and children working and learning together
- Observation-based assessment of the child's learning
- Significance of the development of symbol use

These principles form the foundation of a strong philosophy of learning which promotes effective delivery of the curriculum and the best possible opportunities for children. As one of Froebel's Occupations cooking has a key role to play.

Reflective questions and practical actions

- Consider the seven design principles of the Scottish Curriculum. How can these be used to enhance and extend your own practice?
- Reflect on the context of your early years setting. Do you provide opportunities for cooking? If so, how can these be developed further? If not, can you identify a possible starting point?
- Identify the challenges of developing cooking within your establishment. How might these be overcome?

Introductory reading

Kahn, J. (undated) *More than Cooking*. Booklet on cookery available from London: BAECE: Early Education, and National Children's Bureau.

Further reading

Brown, B. (2004) *Celebrating Diversity: Inclusion in Practice*. London: Persona Doll Training.

Contini, M. and Irvine, P. (1999) *Easy Peasy*. London: Ebury Press.

Lane, J. (2008) *Young Children and Racial Justice: Taking Action for Racial Equality in the Early Years – Understanding the Past, Thinking about the Present, Planning for the Future*. London: National Children's Bureau.

CHAPTER 12

BRINGING TOGETHER FROEBELIAN PRINCIPLES AND PRACTICES

TINA BRUCE

A great deal of practice is handed down from one generation of practitioners to the next. Often this is done without articulating and analysing the reasons why a particular way of presenting or offering experiences to children is habitual. When this happens too often or too much, practice gets into a rut and becomes ossified.

Sometimes the reverse occurs. Practitioners might attend courses, and become infused with a new idea for their practice. This might not connect with the rest of their practice, and might be a matter of fashion, here today and gone tomorrow.

A framework for early childhood practice needs to have inner logic, and coherence. Otherwise one aspect might contradict another. But it also needs to be capable of change so that practice is updated, taking in the diversity that is a rich part of the cultural contexts in which it takes place.

Froebel's approach gives both. The principles give important navigational tools in the complex worlds of early childhood practices today. What is good practice in one setting will not suit another. What is right for one child would be wrong for another. Tools of this kind help to change, repair, mend, replace, modify, adapt and renew the practice that exists.

Education is a continual journey from birth to death

One of the important Froebelian principles (Bruce, 2011a) is that education is a lifelong process. Childhood, therefore is an important part of life, and not just a preparation for adulthood.

Education is about the relationship with self, others and the universe – interconnectedness

Throughout the book there has been emphasis on the way each child is unique, and needs respect and love. Relationships with other people, especially those with whom the child lives are central if children are to live fulfilled lives. This opens the way for practitioners to constantly strive to work at their best with a diverse range of children, each unique. Some children have special educational needs, some speak several languages, some are gifted in dance or music or mathematics, some read earlier than others, some live in minority groups, with a wide diversity of cultures, others live in rural settings, or urban situations, rich, or in poverty, with parents who have a range of skills and education, or in care or foster homes, with little stability in their lives, exposed to criminals, abused, constantly changing, escaping war zones, experiencing ill health.

The practice will need to change according to the child, the context, the need, but the principle holds that each child should be respected as a unique individual, linked with others and helped in forming good relationships.

Relationship with the universe

There has been great emphasis on relationship with nature and the developing symbolic understandings and behaviour of young children in the book, together with consideration of the way the play of children opens up possibilities for the highest levels of learning, freeing children from the here and now. To say this is a spiritual activity in the child is to use a word that is contentious and means different things to different people, depending on whether they are theists or non-theists. But it is not contentious to suggest that it is important to encourage children to consider aspects of their lives which go beyond their immediate experiences in ways which carry deep and lasting meanings for them. Being able to focus in detail on a beetle in the garden, to listen to a sad song and to catch that feeling and, in doing so, connect with a composer, to dance so that a group feeling and sophisticated coming together is felt, to gaze at the sea, to run through long grass, to listen to the silence in the air when it has freshly snowed, to walk in moonlight and see shadows, to cuddle a kitten that is frightened and feel the purring begin. These are early ways in which children begin to relate to the vastness of the universe.

The practitioner and parent work with the whole child (the principle of unity is an aspect of this)

The principle of unity, which includes connectedness helps practitioners to find ways forward and to see the child as a whole person, with feelings, ideas, thoughts, relationships, a sense of identity and a physical self. This principle also connects children to the people with whom they live (usually family), community and the universe itself. The different aspects of experience also become interwoven and interconnected through unity. Nature, gifts, occupations, song, dance, the visual arts, drama, literature, mathematics, time space and reasons all contribute different strands so that children bring these together and develop knowledge of history, geography and other subjects in an integrated, connected way.

Play is the highest form of learning, and helps children to apply what they learn in an integrated way

Play and language are part of the integrating mechanisms which help children to transform experience through the senses and their movements onto a more abstract level with symbolic possibilities. Detailed attention has been given in the book to the important contribution play makes to the development of learning. Language and a vast range of symbolic learning, including language development, are also emphasised.

Children should be supported in developing autonomous learning

Helping children to become autonomous, so that they learn to think and have rich intellectual lives is a powerful Froebelian principle. As we have seen throughout this book, this is a far cry from letting children do as they wish. Because the child is part of a larger whole, that would not be acceptable. But analysing, discussing, planning how things might be, or could have been, helps children to become imaginative, creative and problem generators and solvers.

Autonomy also means that children know how to find and ask for the help they need, and when to do things for themselves.

Self-discipline is the most powerful form of controlling behaviour

Froebel did not focus on faults and deficits in people, and especially not in children. He built on the intrinsic and natural desire of babies, toddlers and young children to participate in family and community life positively. He recognised that self-discipline is the result. Children who are able to discuss, and unpick what goes right or wrong in situations, and who plan with others what to do about difficult situations (who should have the last sweet?) do not constantly turn to higher authority to tell them what to think or do. They are more considerate of others, and this is reflected in their behaviour. The central message of his principle is that children need freedom with guidance. He took the view that behind every bad act is a good intention, and that it is the task of the adult to seek out and identify the good intention and to work with that.

Education should begin where the learner is

As well as the cultural context in which children are brought up, and the strong emphasis on the importance of this and a sense of their community, and how in turn that is linked to the wider world, and even the universe, Froebel also emphasised the crucial role of biology in a child's development. His fascination with the development of the hand and body movements, the transformation of play from the sensory and movement play, to the literal play, to the symbolic pretend and imaginative creativity of play are examples. There is no sense in teaching children what we think they ought to know. There is sense in helping children to learn (teaching) children what they naturally find interesting, which causes a sensible level of effort without disheartening struggle which puts them off, and which encourages them to develop dispositions for lifelong learning.

Practitioners, working with other people's children, need to be well-educated observers, well trained and informed about the development and learning (curriculum and pedagogy) of children

Adults who are good observers, and able to tune into a child's biological and social, cultural and community needs will be powerful educators.

This can be summarised (Kalliala, 2004: 124) as:

- sensitivity to the children's play and the child's culture
- informed observation of play and child development
- knowing the world of children and the community.

At every stage (point of development) be that stage

There will be particular times when children are particularly fascinated by and interested in particular things. They need the time and personal space and help to focus on their interests, from which they will learn deeply, provided everything in the learning environment indoors and outdoors is carefully thought through and presented with educational possibilities. The principle here is that practitioners need to begin where the child is in their learning, rather than where they ought to be. Children need the right help at the right time in the right way.

Children need to spend time with reflective parents and practitioners

Families should not feel isolated in bringing up their children. They should feel supported and part of communities, linked to the wider world. An important impact of Froebelian principles on practice today is that no two Froebelians create early childhood settings or home learning settings, or family lives, which are prescribed in their practice. Froebelian practice cannot be standardised into a method. If this happened, the practice would not be Froebelian any more.

Froebelian principles: navigational tools which guide early childhood practice

In this book the different authors have drawn upon Froebelian principles which guide their practice today. They do not repeat and hold fast to the Froebelian practice of the past. In this way, for example, new technology is incorporated into the practice thoughtfully and with care. It is the Froebelian principles (not received method and practice) which continue to serve as navigational instruments and which guide practice into unknown futures and new forms.

Reflective question

In the Introduction to the book, the question was raised whether you, the reader, are aware of the educational, philosophical and theorietical influences that support and guide your practice. Having read this book, you may or may not find that you are instinctively a Froebelian, but can you articulate why you might or might not be?

Introductory reading

Using the Internet, seek out the early childhood frameworks of the countries of the UK, and other countries which have a written document developed nationally. Can you make any links with Froebelian principles of practice?

Further reading

Miller, L. and Pound, L. (eds) (2010) *Theories and Approaches to Learning in the Early Years*. London: Sage Publications.

INTEGRATED BOOK LIST AND BIBLIOGRAPHY

Allen, M. (Lady Allen of Hurtwood) (1968) *Planning for Play*. London: Thames and Hudson.

Anon. (1910) 'A fortnight's holiday spent at Westgate by forty-six children of the Michaelis Free Kindergarten', *The Link* (1): 16–18.

Athey, C. (1990) *Extending Thought in Young Children: A Parent–Teacher Partnership*. London: Paul Chapman Publishing.

Ball, D., Gill, T. and Spiegal, B. (2008) *Managing Risk in Play Provision: Implementation Guide*. Nottingham: Department for Children, Schools and Families, and Department for Culture, Media and Sport.

Bilton, H. (1998) *Outdoor Play in the Early Years, Management and Innovation*. London: David Fulton.

Bilton, H. (2002) *Outdoor Play in the Early Years*. London: Fulton.

Bloom, A. (2010) '£200K: true value of top reception teachers', *Times Educational Supplement*, 10 August.

Bowen, H.C. (1897) *Froebel and Education through Self-Activity*. New York: Charles Scribner.

Bradburn, E. (1989) *Margaret McMillan: Portrait of a Pioneer*. London: Routledge.

Brehony, K.J. (2000) 'English revisionist Froebelians and schooling of the urban poor', in M. Hilton and P. Hirsch (eds), *Practical Visionaries: Women, Education and Social Progress 1790–1930*. Harlow: Pearson Education.

Brehony, K.J. (2001) *The Origins of Nursery Education: Friedrich Froebel and the English System, Vol 4 Friedrich Froebel's Education by Development*. Trans. J. Jarvis, London and New York: Routledge.

Bretherick, H. (ed.) (2004) *Sound Foundation – a Music Handbook for Early Years*. Croydon: Croydon Early Years and Croydon Music Service

Broadie, E. (2007) *The Scottish Enlightenment*. Edinburgh: Birlinn.

Brosterman, N. (1997) *Inventing Kindergarten*. London: Harry N. Abrams.

Brown, B. (2004) *Celebrating Diversity: Inclusion in Practice*. London: Persona Doll Training.

Bruce, T. (1991) *Time to Play in Early Childhood Education*. London: Hodder and Stoughton.

Bruce, T. (2002) *Learning through Play: Babies, Toddlers and the Foundation Stage*. London: Hodder and Stoughton.

Bruce, T. (2004) *Developing Learning in Early Childhood*. London: Paul Chapman Publishing.

Bruce, T. (2009) 'Learning through Play: Froebelian principles and their practice today', *Early Childhood Practice: The Journal for Multi-Professional Partnerships*, 10 (2): 59–73.

Bruce, T., McNair, L. and Wyn Siencyn, S. (2008) *I Made a Unicorn! Open-ended Play with Blocks and Simple Materials*. Robertsbridge: Community Playthings.

Bruce, T. (2011a) *Early Childhood Education*. 4th edn. London: Hodder Arnold.

Bruce, T. (2011b) *Learning through Play: For Babies, Toddlers and Young Children*. 2nd edn. London: Hodder Arnold.

Bruce, T. (2011c) 'All about Froebel', *Nursery World*, 7 April: 15–19.

Bruce, T. (2011d) *Cultivating Creativity: Babies, Toddlers and Young Children*, 2nd edn. London: Hodder Education.

Bruce, T. (ed.) (2010) *Early Childhood: A Student Guide*. 2nd edn. London: Sage Publications.

Bruce, T. and McNair, L. (2009) *I Made a Unicorn*. Robertsbridge: Community Playthings.

Bruce, T. and Spratt, J. (2011) *Essentials of Literacy from 0 – 7: A Whole-child Approach to Communication, Language and Literacy*. 2nd edn. London: Sage Publications.

Bruce, T., Meggitt, C. and Grenier, J. (2010) *Childcare and Education*. 5th edn. London: Hodder.

Bruhlmeier, A. (2010) *Head, Heart and Hand. Education in the Spirit of Pestalozzi*. Cambridge: Sophia Books.

Bundy, A., Luckett, T., Tranter, P., Naughton, A., Wyver, S., Razen, J. and Spies, G. (2009), The risk is that there is no risk: a simple, innovative intervention to increase children's activity levels', *International Journal of Early Years Education*, 17(1): 33–45

Caillois, R. (2001) *Man, Play and Games*. Trans. M. Barash. Urbana, IL: University of Illinois Press.

Cass-Beggs, B. (1980) *Your Baby Needs Music*. Harlow: Pearson Education.

Cass-Beggs, B. and Cass-Beggs, M. (1986) *Folk Lullabies.* Harlow: Pearson Education.

Claxton, G. (1999) *Wise Up: The Challenge of Life-Long Learning*. London: Bloomsbury.

Clay, M. (1986) *The Patterning of Complex Behaviour.* 3rd edn. Auckland: Heinemann.

Community Playthings (2008) *I Made a Unicorn! Open-ended Play with Blocks and Simple Materials.* Robertsbridge, E. Sussex: Community Playthings

Contini, M. and Irvine, P. (1999) *Easy Peasy.* London: Ebury Press

Cooke, T. (1994) *So Much*. London: Walker Books

Dweck, C. (2000) *Self Theories: Their Role in Motivation, Personality and Development*. Hove: Psychology Press.

Elfer, P. and Grenier, J. (2010) 'Personal, social and emotional development', in T. Bruce (ed.), *Early Childhood: A Student Guide*. London: Sage Publications.

Evans, N. (2006) *Tuning into Children*. London: Youth Music.

Evans, N. (2008) *Reflections on Creative Music-making in the Early Years in Sound Progress.* London:

Fjortoft, I. (2004) 'Landscape as playscape. The effects of natural environments on children's play and motor development', *Children Youth and Environments*, 14(2).

Froebel, F. (1843) *Mutter und Koselieder. (Mother's Songs, Games and Stories by Friedrich Froebel.* Trans. into English by Frances and Emily Lord in 1920. London: William Rice.)

Froebel, F. (1861) *The Pedagogics of the Kindergarten.* (Edited by W. Lange in 2001.) New York: D. Appleton.

Froebel, F. (1895) *The Mottoes and Commentaries of Friedrich Froebel's Mother Play*. H.R. Eliot and S.E. Blow (eds). New York: D. Appleton.

Froebel, F. (1895) *The Mottoes and Commentaries of Friedrich Froebel's Mother Play*. (Edited by H.R. Eliot and S.E. Blow (eds) in 2004). Honolulu: Honolulu University Press.

Froebel, F. (1896) *Education by Development*.

Froebel, F. (1926) *The Education of Man*.

Froebel, F. *Plan of an Institution for the Education of the Poor in the Canton of Berne,* in Lilley (1967) *Friedrich Froebel: A Selection from his Writings.* London: Cambridge University Press.

Gadhuk, K. (2011) Royal College of Speech and language Therapists in 'Sociable buggies make their mark', on The Baby Website (previously on Talk to Your Baby website).

Geoghegan, L. (2002) *Singing and Rhymes for Early Years.* Glasgow: The National Youth Choir of Scotland.

Gerhardt, S. (2007) *Why Love Matters.* London: Routledge.

Gill, T. (2007) *No Fear: Growing Up in a Risk Averse Society*. London: Calouste Gulbenkian Foundation.

Goddard Blythe, S. (2004) *The Well-Balanced Child: Movement and Early Learning.* Stroud: Hawthorn Press.

Goddard Blythe, S. (2011) *The Genius of Natural Childhood.* Stroud: Hawthorn Press.

Goouch, K. (2007) 'Parents' voices: a conversation with parents of pre-school children', in K. Goouch and A. Lambirth (eds), *Understanding Phonics and the Teaching of Reading: Critical Perspectives.* Maidenhead: Open University Press/McGraw-Hill.

Gopnik, A., Meltzoff, A. and Kuhl, P. (1999) *How Babies Think.* London: Weidenfeld and Nicolson

Goswami, U. (2007) 'Learning to read across languages: the role of phonics and synthetic phonics', in K. Goouch and A. Lambirth (eds), *Understanding Phonics and the Teaching of Reading: Critical Perspectives.* Maidenhead: Open University Press/McGraw-Hill.

Greenland, P. (2006) 'Physical development', in T. Bruce (ed.) *Early Childhood: A Guide for Students.* London: Sage Publications.

Greenland, P. (2010) 'Physical development', in T. Bruce (ed.) *Early Childhood: A Guide for Students.* 2nd edn. London: Sage Publications.

Gura, P. (ed.) (1992) *Exploring Learning: Young Children and Blockplay.* London: Paul Chapman Publishing.

Hardy, L. (1913) *Diary of a Free Kindergarten*, London: Gay and Hancock.

Harrison, C. (2007) 'Music for all – how do we make it a reality?', in H. Coll and J. Finney (eds), *Ways into Music, Making Every Child's Music Matter.* Matlock: National Association of Music Editors.

Harrison, E. (1895) *A Study of Child Nature from the Kindergarten Standpoint.* New York and London: Garland (Originally published by the Chicago Kindergarten College in 1895.)

Holmes, J. (1993) *John Bowlby and Attachment Theory.* London: Routledge.

Isaacs, S. (1930) *Intellectual Growth in Young Children.* London: Routledge and Kegan Paul.

Isaacs, S. (1933) *Social Development in Young Children.* London: Routledge and Kegan Paul.

Isaacs, S. (1970) *Intellectual Growth in Young Children.* London: Routledge.

Johnson, H. (1933) 'The art of blockbuilding', reprinted in E.F. Provenzo Jr and A. Brett, (1983) *The Complete Block Book.* Syracuse, NY: Syracuse University Press.

Kahn, J. (2003) *More than Cooking: Developing Children's Learning through Cooking.* London: Early Education. www.early-education.org.uk

Kalliala, M. (2006) *Play Culture in a Changing World.* Maidenhead: Open University Press.

Kloep, M. and Hendry, L (2007) '"Over-protection, over-protection, over-protection!" Young people in modern Britain', *Psychology of Education Review*, 31(2): 4–8.

Knight, S. (2009) *Forest School and Outdoor Learning in the Early Years.* London: Sage Publications.

Knight, S. (2011) *Risk and Adventure in Early Years Outdoor Play. Learning from Forest Schools*. London: Sage Publications.

Kuhlman, K. and Schweinhart, L. (1999) *Music, Movement and Timing*. Ypsilanti, MI: High Scope Educational Research Foundation.

Lane, J. (2008) *Young Children and Racial Justice: Taking Action for Racial Equality in the Early Years – Understanding the Past, Thinking about the Present, Planning for the Future*. London: National Children's Bureau.

Lascarides, V.C. and Blythe, H.F. (2000) *History of Early Childhood Education*. London: Falmer Press.

Liebschner, J. (1992) *A Child's Work: Freedom and Guidance in Froebel's Educational Theory and Practice*. Cambridge: Lutterworth.

Lilley, I. (ed.) (1967) *Friedrich Froebel: A Selection from his Writings*. London: Cambridge University Press.

Lindon, J. (2011) *Too Safe for Their Own Good? Helping Children Learn about Risk And Skills*. 2nd edn. London: National Children's Bureau.

Little, H. (2006) 'Children's risk taking behaviour: implications for early childhood policy and practice', *International Journal of Early Years Education*, 14(2): 141–54.

Lyschinska, M. J. (1922) *Henriette Schrader Breymann: Life and letters*. Unpublished and unpaginated translation in manuscript of M. J. Lyschinska, *Henriette Schrader Breymann. Ihr Leben*. Berlin and Leipzig: Walter de Gruyter.

Malloch, S. and Trevarthen, C. (2009) *Communicative Musicality: Exploring the Basis of Human Companionship*. Oxford: Oxford University Press.

Matterson, E., (1969) *This Little Puffin*. London : Penguin Books.

Matthews, J. (2003) *Drawing and Painting: Children and Visual Representation*. 2nd edn. London: Paul Chapman Publishing.

McCann, P. and Young, F.A. (1982) *Samuel Wilderspin and the Infant School Movement*. London: Croom Helm.

McMillan, M. (1919) *The Nursery School*. London: Dent.

McMillan, M. (1930) *The Nursery School*. London: Dent.

McMillan, M. (n.d.) *What the Open-Air Nursery School Is*. London: Labour Party.

McNair, L. (2007) 'A developmental project in the garden: how Froebelian is it?', *Early Childhood Practice: The Journal for Multi-Professional Partnerships*, 9 (1): 26–42.

McNicol, R. (2000) *Music Explorer for Infants*. London: London Symphony Orchestra.

McVicar, E. (2007) *Doh Ray Me, When Ah wis Wee: Scots Children's Songs and Rhymes*. Edinburgh: Birlinn.

Michaelis Free Kindergarten. *Annual Report 1928*, London.

Michaelis Free Kindergarten (1908) *Prospectus*, London.

Michaelis, E. and Keatley Moore, H. (eds) (2010) *Froebel's Letters on the Kindergarten*. (First published in 1891. Translated by Hermann Poesche in 1891.) Whitefish, MT: Kessinger.

Miller, L. and Pound, L. (eds) (2010) *Theories and Approaches to Learning in the Early Years.* London: Sage Publications.

Mithen, S. (2005) *The Singing Neanderthals.* Cambridge, MA: Harvard University Press.

Mollenhauer, K. (1991) 'Finger play: a pedagogical reflection', *Phenomenology and Pedagogy*, 9: 286–300.

Morrow, J (2000) *Music–Early Years Activities to Promote Children's Creative Development.* Dunstable: Belair Publications.

Murray, E.R. (1903) 'That symmetrical paper folding and symmetrical work with Gifts are a waste of time for both students and children', *Child Life*, 17: 14–18.

Nylan, B., Ferris, J. and Dunn, L. (2008) 'Mindful hands, gestures as language: listening to children', *Early Years: An International Journal of Research and Development*, 28 (1): 73–80.

Ouvry, M. (2000) *Exercising Muscles and Minds: Outdoor play and the Early Years Curriculum.* London: National Early Years Network.

Ouvry, M. (2003) *Sounds Like Playing.* London: BAECE.

Ouvry, M. (2004) *Sounds like Playing.* London: British Association for Early Childhood Education.

Papousek, H. (1984) 'To the evolution of human musicality and musical education', in I. Deliege (ed.), *Proceedings of the 3rd International Conference for Music Perception and Cognition.* Liege: ESCOM.

Pellegrini, T. (1998) *Horizon*, BBC 2 television programme, 5 November..

Poulson, E., music by Roeske, C. (1921) *Finger Plays for Nursery and Kindergarten.* Norwood, MA: Norwood Press. (Originally printed in Boston in 1893 by Lothrop, Lee and Shepard Co.)

Pound, L. and Harrison, C. (2003) *Supporting Musical Development in the Early Years.* Buckingham: Open University Press.

Prufer, J. (1927) *Friedrich Froebel.* Leipzig: Mutter und Koselieder.

Reed, L. (1945) 'Miss Lawrence and the early days of the Notting Hill Nursery School', *The Link*.

Report of the Michaelis Free Kindergarten, (1908) *Child Life*, 10(39): 110.

Rowland, P. (2004) Personal communication, interview 3 April, London.

Sandseter, E. (2007) 'Categorising risky play: how can we identify risk taking in children's play?', *European Early Childhood Research*, 15(2): 237–52.

Sandseter, E. (2009) 'Children's expressions of exhilaration and fear in risky play', *Contemporary Issues in Early Childhood*, 10(2): 92–106.

Scottish Executive, Learning and Teaching Scotland (2007) *Taking Learning Outdoors: Partnerships for Excellence.* Glasgow: Learning and Teaching Scotland.

Scottish Executive, Learning and Teaching Scotland (2009) *Curriculum for Excellence 3–18.* Glasgow: Learning and Teaching Scotland.

Scottish Teachers TV 'Learning and Teaching Scotland: filmed conversations with experts – early years', www.lt.scotland.org.uk/earlylearning.

Somers Town Nursery School Annual Report, 1913, 1914, London.

Sorace, A. (2010) 'Bilingualism matters', lecture given to Edinburgh and Lothians branch of British Association for Early Childhood Education, 29 April.

Spinka, M., Newberry, R. and Bekoff, M. (2001) 'Mammalian play: training for the unexpected', *The Quarterly Review of Biology*, 76(2): 141–68.

Spratt, J. (2007) 'Finger rhymes: why are they important?', *Early Childhood Practice: The Journal for Multi-Professional Partnerships,* 9(1): 43–54.

Stephenson, A. (2003) 'Physical risk taking: dangerous or endangered?', *Early Years* 23(1): 35–43.

Stokes (1933) 'A short history of Somers Town Nursery School', *The Link*, (23): 33–4.

Sutherland, K. (2009) *Katie's Coo: Scots Rhymes for Wee Folk*. Edinburgh: Itchy Coo.

The *Scotsman* Digital Archive (1930) Scotsman.com, 25 September, 108 Holyrood House, Edinburgh EH8 8AS, tel. no. 0131 620 8620.

Tickell, C. (2011) *The Early Years: Foundations for Life, Health and Learning: An Independent Report on the Early Years Foundation Stage to her Majesty's Government.* (Tickell Review.) London: Department of Education.

Tovey, H. (2007) *Playing Outdoors: Spaces and Places, Risk and Challenge*. Maidenhead: Open University Press.

Tovey, H. (2010) 'Playing on the edge: perceptions of risk and danger in outdoor play', in P. Broadhead, J. Howard and E. Woods (eds), *Play and Learning in the Early Years: from Research to Practice*. London. Sage Publications.

Tower Hamlets (1997) *Making Music from Early Years to Key Stage 2.* London: Learning Design.

Trevarthen, C. (1989), 'Signs before speech', in T.A. Sebeok, and J. Umiker Sebeok (eds), *The Semiotic Web*. Berlin: Walter de Gruyter.

Trevarthen, C. (2004) 'Introduction', in T. Bruce, (ed.), *Developing Learning in Early Childhood*. London: Paul Chapman Publishing.

Vygotsky, L. (1978) *Mind in Society: The Development of Higher Psychological Processes.* London and Cambridge, MA: Harvard University Press.

Welter, V. M. (2002) *BIOPOLIS: Patrick Geddes the City of Life*. London: Massachusetts Institute of Technology.

Weston, P. (2002) *The Froebel Educational Institute: The Origins and History of the College*. Roehampton: University of Surrey Roehampton.

Whinnett, J. (2006) 'Froebelian practice today: the search for unity', *Early Childhood Practice: The Journal for Multi-Professional Partnerships*, 8(2): 58–80.

White, J. (1907) *The Educational Ideas of Froebel*. London: University Tutorial Press.

Whitehead, M. (2009) *Supporting Language and Literacy Development in the Early Years*. 2nd edn. Maidenhead: Open University Press/McGraw-Hill.

Whitehead, M. (2010) *Language and Literacy in the early Years 0–7* (4th edn) London: Sage Publications.

Wiggin, K.D. and Smith, N.A. (1986) *Kindergarten Principles and Practice.* London: Gay and Bird.

Wood, V. (1983) *Music and Song.* BBC radio programme.

Woodhead, M., Faulkner, D. and Littleton, K. (1998) *Cultural Worlds of Early Childhood.* Maidenhead: Open University Press

Young, S. (2003) *Music with the Under Fours.* London: Routledge Falmer.

Young, S. (2007) 'Digi-kids age 5: new technologies and the first years of music education', in *Ways Into Music – Making Every Child's Music Matter.* London.

Young, S. and Glover, J. (1998) *Music in the Early Years.* Brighton: Falmer Press.

INDEX

A

Active learning xii, 7, 11, 48, 54, 62, 73, 82, 84, 153
   See also self activity
Adventure 43, 45, 56, 51, 53, 72, 74
Adult role 59, 63, 66, 79, 125, 146, 148, 153
   See also Freedom with guidance, self discipline, behaviour, first hand experience, language development, environment
Autonomy 11, 15, 30, 54, 157, 158

B

Behaviour 22, 66
   See also family, inner motivation, inner life, relationships
Bilingual 126
   See also EAL, diversity, culture, symbolic life
Books 87, 89, 139, 148, 150–1

C

Cause and effect 15
   See also reasons

Challenge 43, 44, 46, 49, 72, 74
Child-centred 79
   See also unique child
Clay 132–3, 58
   See also Occupations
Community 6, 15, 17–18, 21, 26–7, 42, 53, 61, 67, 82–3, 92–3, 96, 99, 114, 135, 153
   See also diversity, culture, universe, wider world, parents, family
Concentration 14
   See also involved, focussed
Construction 26
   See also Gifts and Occupations
Cooking 1, 37, 138, 144
   See also Occupations
Co-operative play 124
   See also social life, relationships, play
Core and radial schema 122–4, 130
   See also Gifts and Occupations, space
Countryside 78
   See also wider world, nature
Creativity 14, 47, 50, 128, 158
   See also Gifts and Occupations

Curriculum for Excellence (Scotland) xii,
37–40, 134, 148, 148–50, 152
Curriculum frameworks for the UK 160

D
Diversity 2–3, 10, 84, 156
See also men in the early childhood
workforce, EAL
Drawing 126–7, 129, 133, 142–3
See also Occupations, symbolic life,
graphics/mark making

E
Educationally worthwhile experiences 23
EAL 29, 137, 150
Ecological 41, 67, 92
See also nature
Embedded Froebelian practice 1
Enclosure schema 125, 129
See also Gifts, space
Enlightenment 5–6
Environment 54, 127, 148
See also autonomy, freedom with
guidance, first hand experience,
active learning, physical
environment
Experience
See first hand experience
Exploration/experimentation 72, 116,
125, 141, 144
See also active learning
Expressive arts
See arts
Eyes 82–4, 97, 104, 114, 139, 144
See also hands, active learning, voice,
language development

F
Family 14–5, 17–8, 24–5, 27, 119,
135, 153
See also partnership, grandparents,
community
Family songs 81–93
Features of play
See play
Feet 44, 85
See also hands, voice, music
Finger rhymes/plays 95, 100, 101–3, 111
See also Rhyme and Rhythm, Mother
Songs

First hand experience 7, 13, 4, 61, 77,
131–2, 142, 144, 148, 153
See also active learning, environment
Focussed
(*See* concentration and involved)
Forest school 1–2, 21, 59, 63–4
Freedom with guidance xii, 15, 22
See also inner motivation
inner life, relationships, family,
behaviour, self discipline
Friendships 125, 140–1
See also social life, relationships
Froebel blockplay Collaborative research
Project 26
Froebel Certificate Courses, Canterbury
Christchurch, Edinburgh, Roehampton
Universities vii–x
Froebel's life 2, 21–2
Froebelian principles xiii, 2, 6–7, 27, 41,
54, 67, 78, 93, 105, 119, 134, 143, 153,
155, 159
Froebelian Research Nursery school 25–6

G
Games 87, 111
See also Movement games, peekaboo
Garden 1, 8, 11, 25, 40, 70–1, 149
See also outdoor, nature
Gifts 2, 74, 121, 128
See also mathematics
Grandparents 19, 20, 82, 99
See also family, relationships
Graphics 127, 129, 142–3
See also drawing, occupations
Groups of children 62
See also social life, relationships,
adult role

H
Hands 44, 96–9, 104, 111, 119, 144, 158
See also finger rhymes/plays, eyes, voice,
music, Mother Songs
Healing 63–4
See also health
Health 76, 144–5, 149–50
High expectations 53
Hoffmeister, Wilhelmine 3
Holistic 1, 41, 60, 67, 93, 119, 134, 144, 153
Home learning 2
See also family

Horizontal trajectory schema 1, 32, 122–4, 126
  See also Gifts, space, occupations, weaving

I
Imitation 93
  See also Symbolic life
Inclusion 150
  See also diversity
Individual child
  See unique child
Inner life 14, 22, 27, 58, 128
  See also behaviour, relationships, family, freedom with guidance, self-discipline
Intrinsic motivation 11, 65
Involved
  See focussed, concentration

J
Jena 2
Johnson, Harriet 121
  See also Gifts/wooden blocks

K
Kant 7, 15, 24
  See also time, space and reasons
Keilhau 3
Key person
  See relationships
Kindergarten 3, 34, 50, 60, 65, 69–72, 76, 95

L
Langethal 3
Language development 79, 87, 90–1, 147, 157
Levin, Louise 3
Links
  See Unity of learning, whole child
Literacy 150
  See also language development, talk, drawing, play, stories and poems, rhyme and rhythm
Lullabies 82, 90

M
Mathematics 124, 140, 147–8, 150–1, 156
McMillan, Margaret 35, 48, 76–7
Middendorff 3

Montessori, Maria 15
Mother Songs 3, 9, 91, 95, 99, 108, 110–1
Music 81, 88–90, 92, 96, 109–10, 116–8
  See also community and culture

N
Nature 1, 7, 9, 52, 57–9, 61, 64, 70, 72, 144, 149, 153, 157
  See also ecological, garden, forest school, countryside, wider world
Network of Froebelian practice 6
Numeracy
  See mathematics
Nursery schools 35

O
Observation 30, 40, 57–8, 69, 81, 96, 107, 110, 121, 134, 138, 149, 153, 158–9
Occupations 2, 12–3, 74, 121, 126, 131–2, 144–5, 154
  See also symbolic life, cooking, paper pricking, tessellations, printing, weaving, sewing, clay, shape, paper folding
Open-ended 47, 54
Opposites (law of) 117, 119
Outdoors 4, 24, 40, 43, 69, 74–5, 79
Owen, Robert 69–70

PQ
Paper folding/pricking/printing 131
  See also Occupations
Parent partnership, involvement 24–5, 73, 86, 114, 147, 149
  See also family
Past, present and future 9
  See also symbolic life of the child
Persistence 74
  See also inner motivation involved, concentration, focussed
Personal space 66
Pestalozzi 3
Planning 38–40, 66, 147
Play 13–4, 57, 62, 65–7, 93, 115, 119, 126, 135, 152–3
Poems
  See stories and poems
Preparing children for adult life 41, 153, 156

Pretending 9, 14
  See also symbolic life
Principles
  See Froebelian principles
Problem-solving 74

R
Readiness for adult life/school 41, 159
Reasons (cause and effect) 125
  See also Kant
Recipe book
  See books, cooking
Relationships 19, 63, 112, 147, 149
  See also social life
Religious freedom 6, 152
Rhyme and rhythm, 9, 90–3, 100, 117
Risk xii, 45, 7, 49, 51, 53, 64–5
Role of the adult
  See adult role
Role play
  See symbolic life, pretend
Romantic 1
Rousseau, Jacques 18
Rules 1

S
Schemas 126, 135
  See also vertical, horizontal trajectory,
    enclosure, core and radial
Science 151
  See also nature
Seasons 5, 29, 31–3
  See also nature, garden
Self activity 5, 7, 14
  See also active learning
Self discipline 23, 25, 27
  See also behaviour, inner motivation,
    inner life, relationships, family
Sewing
  See Occupations
Shape
  See also space, Occupations
Sight
  See eyes

Social life 11, 20, 63, 112
  See also relationships, family, groups,
    adult role
Song 9, 82–4, 89–2, 99, 110, 112–4, 128–9
Sounds 96
Steiner, Rudolf 15
Stories and poems 9, 118, 128–9, 140–1,
    143, 147–8, 152
Symbolic life 7, 9, 93, 104, 126, 129–30,
    132–3, 140–2, 153, 157–8

T
Talking 9
  See language development,
    symbolic life
Tessellations
  See Occupations
Time, space and reasons 54, 157
  See also Kant
Trajectory schemas 126, 130, 133
  See also schemas

U
Unique child 41, 79, 93, 99, 134, 156–7
Unity of learning 2, 7–8, 105, 153, 156–7
Universe 1, 4–5, 7, 14, 156

V
Vertical schema 122–4, 126
Voice 82, 111, 114, 117

WXYZ
Weaving 132
  See also Occupations
Wider world 1, 4, 6, 17, 71–2, 75, 78, 151–2
  See also diversity
Wilderspin, Samuel 69
Wild site 65
  See also forest school
Whole child 1, 5, 7–8, 15, 50, 54, 63
Wooden blockplay 2, 11–2, 26
  See also Gifts
Workshop experience
  See Occupations